GOD'S LISTENING
Prayer for Today

BY ANITA WAMBLE

Copyright © 2016 by Anita Wamble
Published by Refined Concepts, Fort Washington, MD

Printed and bound in the U.S.A.

www.anitawambleministries.com
www.refinedconcepts.net

I dedicate this book and journal to my mother
Syble L. Patterson, my grandmothers Ruth G. McNeil
and Rayella Satterfield Jones and Edna Mae Patterson,
my step-mother. These women taught me the power of prayer
and the necessity of trusting and obeying God.

ACKNOWLEDGMENTS

First, I want to thank my Lord and Savior Jesus Christ, without whom nothing I do would be possible. My husband, Rev. Marvin Wamble and my children Alicia Williams, Julian and Jenise Wamble, thank you for all your love and support.

Renee Holtz-Sharp, my publisher, website manager, videographer and friend. This would not have been possible with you being in my corner. Kerry-Ann Powell, my accountability partner and friend, thank you for pressing me and keeping me on track.

Jeannette Sabathia, who believed in me when I didn't believe in myself.

There are many more people who loved, helped and supported me through the competition this project. Thank you all!

Preface

"And pray in the Spirit on all occasions with all kinds of prayers and requests. With this in mind, be alert and always keep on praying for all the Lord's people" **Ephesians 6:18**

All of us go through difficulties, trials and tribulations. We have to deal with issues like the loss of loved ones, close friendships ending, caring for aging parents or contending with difficult children.

Sometimes, we have to face being laid off from our jobs, losing the family businesses, divorce, spousal abuse or a family member that is returning from a combat zone with mental or emotional issues that are affecting the household.

It is in these times Christians and some non-Christians turn to prayer; we realize that we need to have a little talk with the Master! In fact, for some of us, the only time we talk to God is when we realize that our backs are against the wall and we without God, we won't make it through this situation. Prayer becomes our "go to" place in the midst of our storms.

Prayer should be a part of our daily lives. During the good, the bad or the ugly times of our lives, we should incorporate prayer just like we incorporate food and water.

Our physical bodies need food and water to survive and our spiritual lives needs a relationship with God, through Christ, via the vehicle of prayer in order to survive.

When I talk to people about their prayer lives they usually say, they don't pray on a regular basis because they don't know what to say. Usually, they've heard people praying corporately in their churches, Temples or sanctuaries, and they think they have to pray like them in order to have God hear them. They are so wrong! God wants us to talk to him like he's our best friend. No Elizabethan English required

To help people incorporate prayer into their daily lives Anita Wamble Ministries has been distributing "Prayer for Today" for friends and family since 2009. Over time, we have prayed to God for help in the aftermath of natural and man-made disasters; we've prayed for salvation of friends and family members; health related issues; the economic turnaround of our nations and many other local, national and international issues. The majority of the prayers in this book have been taken from these "Prayer for Today".

In keeping with how most of us pray, the majority of these prayers are self-centered. Most of us pray for ourselves, our circumstances and our problems. We pray for our spouses, children and maybe a friend or two but, really, most of our prayer time is spent on "me, myself and I." Would your attitude about prayer change if you knew there were people all over the world going through the same problems as you? Would you be willing to ask God to do for them what you're asking him to do for you?

In keeping with God's word that ask us to pray for one another, I ask that you consider praying each prayer for yourself and add this phrase, "for someone else who is going through the same thing that I am, I pray that you do for them what I'm asking you to do for me." This way, we will be spreading our prayers to places our feet may not go. Our prayers can abound and make a difference.

I pray that this book of prayers, the companion prayer journal and God's promises booklet will help you increase in your relationship with God Almighty and our savior, Jesus Christ.

My prayer for you is the same prayer that Paul had for the Ephesians:

"For this reason I kneel before the Father, from whom every family in heaven and earth derives its name. I pray that out of his glorious riches he may strengthen you with power through his Spirit in your inner being, so that Christ may dwell in your heart through faith. And I pray that you, being rooted and established in love, may have power, together with all the Lord's holy people, to grasp how wide and long and high and deep is the love of Christ, and to know this love that surpasses knowledge – that you may be filled to the measure of all the fullness of God." Ephesians 3:14 – 19 (NIV)

Living Above Mediocrity, Anita Wamble

CONTENTS

1 Self-Care **1**
Prayers concerning how we care for ourselves physically,
emotionally, financially and spiritually. If we don't care for
ourselves, we can't take care of anyone else or complete our
assignments for the Kingdom of God.

2 Forgiveness **23**
One of the most important aspects of our lives, spiritual and
natural, is to forgive. Prayers to forgive ourselves and others.
Without forgiveness, we will remain locked in the hurt and the pain
of the past.

3 Change **34**
These prayers help us change how we view ourselves, others and
God.

4 Spiritual Growth **52**
These prayers tackle basic truths that we need to incorporate in
our lives in order to become the people God purposed and planned
each of us to be.

5 Family **135**
These prayers are for our spouses, children, family and friends.

6 Community **143**
Prayers for our nation, military, cities, school districts and the
world community.

7 Holidays **167**
The holiday seasons have the potential to be very stressful times.
These prayers were designed to help us remember what is really
important during the holidays.

1 SELF CARE

Father, I find myself dealing with rejection from my past and present: rejection by family, so-called friends and yes, even those in the Body of Christ. I still have scars and hurts that I haven't been able to get over. Often, without warning and at the worst time, my scars and emotional bruises come up and I find myself slipping backwards. I drift into who I was, not being who You have told me I am.

I am so thankful that even if my mother and father reject me, You will never reject me. From today on, when I feel rejected or inferior, I will say of myself what You say about me.

You say I am blessed with all spiritual blessings in the heavenly realm through Jesus Christ. You say I am Your child according to the good pleasure of Your will. You have accepted and redeemed me through the blood of Jesus.

By Your word, I am a wise and prudent person; I am more than an overcomer; I am a partaker in all of Your promises through Christ.

Lord, everything You say about me is true, because everything You say is true. Therefore, I will walk with my head held high in boldness and confidence and say, "I am the Lord's workmanship. I have been fearfully and wonderfully made. Let others reject me, for my Father God loves me completely." Thank you!

In Jesus' name I pray. Amen.

Scripture References:

Psalm 27:10	Ephesians 1:3	Ephesians 1:8
II Peter 1:4	Ephesians 2:10	Psalm 136:2
Psalm 42:11	Ephesians 1:5 – 7	Revelation 12:11
Psalm 33:4	Psalm 139:14	

Today Father, regardless of what is going on, I proclaim that I will not suffer at the hands of the ungodly but, I will say of the Lord, He is my master, my strength, my hope, and my glory. He is the lifter of my head.

You, the Lord God, will protect me when trouble is going on around me. You will not let me stay down even if I stumble and fall. I will rise again.

You Father are the God of all creation. You are my stronghold, my helper and my guide; what can mere man do to me? Things may look bleak and difficult, but I will not allow despair to overtake me. I am more than a conqueror through Jesus Christ. I will proclaim Your Word over my life, situations and circumstances today.

I will remain stable and fixed in my faith. I will be like a tree planted by streams of water. I will not be moved by the things that are going on. I will trust in the Lord with all my heart and lean not to my own understanding.

Father, I ask to hear from You. I know You have heard my cries for help; please answer me and show Yourself strong in my life today.

In Jesus' name I pray. Amen.

Scripture References:

Psalms 140:1 – 3	Psalms 27	Samuels 22:3
Jeremiah 17:8	Psalms 55:1 – 3	Proverbs 24:16
1 Samuel 25:28-30	Psalms 37:1 – 3	
Psalms 17:6	Psalms 119:145	

Father, I give You my time today. Help me to be productive. Help me not to be lazy or a sluggard. Strengthen me to move out and do what You have ordained me to do today.

Let me not waste precious time watching meaningless TV or playing on the computer. Help me monitor my time in such a way that I can be productive and have some down time to enjoy my family, friends and my "me" time.

Father, my time is a valuable commodity that You have given me to fulfill all the tasks of my day, and then to find sweet sleep at the end of my work. My time is not intended to be wasted. Forgive me for squandering my time and help me to move into a new level of time management. Help me manage my time by the tasks You give me to complete and not by my lazy tendencies.

In Jesus' name I pray. Amen.

Scripture References:

Proverbs 13:4	Romans 13:11	Ephesians 5:15 – 18
Psalms 39:4 – 5	Proverbs 10:4	I Corinthians 10:31
Proverbs 26:14 – 16	Proverbs 12:14	
Proverbs 3:24	Psalms 90:12	

Father, every day someone – or some industry – is telling me who I am; how I should feel; what I should do and how I should look. All too often I allow their words to override Your Word in my mind and in my heart. I end up believing their truths rather than affirming myself in The Truth. I end up speaking words of the world system, rather than the words of The Truth.

Your Word says that the power of life and death lies in the tongue. It also says that as I think so am I. Therefore, today I resolve to say about me what You say about me.

You say I am blessed with all spiritual blessings in heavenly places in Christ, because I have been chosen by the Father of all creation to be a child of God. You say I am accepted by You because I am Your workmanship. I am an heir to the promises of God, and I am rooted and grounded in love.

am blessed everywhere I go and victorious in everything I do. I do not concern myself with people's slanderous talk, for they and their words will pass away, but Your words to me – and about me – will never pass away.

Father, Your eyes are upon me, for I have right standing with You. Your ears are attentive to my prayers. Despite what others may say, I declare that everything You say about me in Your Word is true and I will walk therein.

In Jesus' name I pray. Amen.

Scripture References:

Proverbs 18:21	Proverbs 8:32
	Proverbs 23:7 (KJV)

Father, how precious is Your name in all the Earth! How wonderful are Your works in the Earth and in the heavenly realm? My soul is made glad by the knowledge of Your work in my life. I refuse to turn back to what I was or where I was before You changed me. I will cling to You and Your Word today.

Lord, today I want my mind filled with whatever is true, whatever is noble, whatever is right, whatever is pure, whatever is lovely, whatever is admirable—if anything is excellent or praiseworthy—I want to think about such things.

Right now Father God, I want the Spirit of love, joy, peace, patience, kindness, goodness, faithfulness, gentleness, and self-control to enter my life in such a way that everyone who comes in contact with me today will know there is something different about me.

Today, I purpose to allow the words of my mouth and the meditation of my heart to be pleasing in Your sight, for You are my Lord, my Rock and my Redeemer.

In Jesus' name I pray. Amen.

Scripture References:

Psalms 8:1	Galatians 5:22-23
Philippians 4:8	Psalm 19:14

Father, I am so grateful for all the wonderful things You have done for me. You brought me through some times in my life when I thought I'd never make it. You kept me from falling into the hands of the enemy more times than I can count; and if I'm honest, you've saved me from myself on more than a few occasions.

Lord, all those difficult times have caused emotional baggage. I have built up walls and barriers to keep people out so that I don't get hurt any more. I've learned to lie to myself and others so that no one knows how much I ache inside, and I've even tried to convince You that I'm all right. But You know all things, even the deepest hurts that have controlled my life.

Father, today I turn my hurts over to You. I ask You to begin the healing process in my heart, mind and spirit. I ask that You fill the cracks and creases that life has put in my heart and mind with Your Word, Your love, peace, mercy, and grace. I need You, Father. No one else can do this for me. No one else can heal me. No one else can deliver me.

You alone are my healer, my God, my Lord, and my Savior. Rescue me, Lord, from my yesterday.

In Jesus' name I pray. Amen.

Scripture References:

Isaiah 58:8	Proverbs 12:18	Proverbs 15:4
Jeremiah 8:22	Matthew 4:23	
Chronicles 28:15	Proverbs 13:17	
Jeremiah 33:6	Acts 3:16	

Father, if I really think about it and am honest with myself, I have no reason to complain. If I take the time to think about my life, I will notice that the good You have shown me over the course of my days far outweighs the bad.

Even during my bad times, You were working to mature and groom me in an effort to prepare me to become the person You created me to be. Today Father, I will not complain about whatever comes my way. Instead of complaining, I will thank You for Your goodness and Your mercy, which are new to me every morning.

I will take time to consider Your goodness toward me, and I will speak of Your love for me all day long.

In Jesus' name I pray. Amen.

Scripture References:

Lamentations 3:39	Philippians 4:11 – 12	Hebrews 13:5
Matthew 6:25 – 34	I Timothy 6:6-8	

Lord, I know You put everything in its proper place. Unfortunately, I don't always allow my yesterday to stay in the past. Today, I need to move forward and out of all the junk of yesterday. I can't adjust the past to change my today, but I can adjust my attitude today and change my tomorrow.

Father, I need to get out of my rearview mirror and stop lamenting about what was and move forward with what is and what shall be. Tomorrow is not promised to me, but if my tomorrow becomes my today I want it to be the best. And I want to be the best in my tomorrow. I'm tired of being held back and shackled by something I can't do anything about. Free me from my past tense life.

I can't change what happened when I was a child. I can't go back and undo what I perceive as my parents' bad decisions. I can't change the fact that I married the wrong person the first time, nor can I change who my child's mother or father is; and I can't undo the choices my children make, or the bad habits of my mate.

I can stand firmly planted in Your Word, knowing that You have a plan for me: a plan to prosper me, a plan to give me a hope and a future. You have a plan to give me health and healing in every phase of my life. My heart looks up to You for my future tense.

Today, I surrender my yesterday to You, Lord God. I give it all to You: the good, the bad and the ugly. Today I purpose with my whole heart to walk in Your way, being led by Your Spirit, and not succumbing to the tape recorded messages of my yesterday.

In Jesus' name I pray. Amen.

Scripture References:

Ecclesiastes 3:14-16	I Corinthians 13:11	III John 2
Psalms 1:3	Jeremiah 29:11	Psalms 143:10

This is the day that You, Father God, have made and I will rejoice and be glad in it!

Father, I'm going to celebrate myself today. If no one says anything good or positive to me or about me, I will say good and positive things about myself. I am great and mighty in Your sight. There is nothing too difficult for me to grasp, understand and then carry out.

Yes, I've failed in the past. Yes, I've come up short. Yes, I've made bad decisions. And yes, I blow it from time to time. But I thank You for Your grace and mercy. I will fail again, but I will put You first and place my wholehearted trust in You. Then, I will be victorious in everything You set my hands to do. I will conquer every place that You set my feet. Nothing will be impossible for me.

I stand ready to achieve the greatness You have locked in my DNA. I am ready, willing and able to do everything You have purposed me to do.

In Jesus' name I pray. Amen!

Scripture References:

Psalms 118:24   Luke 1:37

Father, this week I pray for balance. Help me correctly balance my days and evenings so that I give my employer whatever they deserve. I will not withhold anything from them that they deserve, just like I don't want them to withhold anything from me that I deserve. Let me render unto them what is rightfully theirs: my time, talents and abilities for the hours I am in their employ.

Help me correctly balance home life, family life, friends, and some quiet time for myself. Help me, Lord, to get the rest, exercise and nourishment I need to in order to fulfill all the duties and responsibilities on my life. Help me, Lord, to balance my life effectively.

In Jesus' name I pray. Amen.

Scripture References:

Matthew 22:21	I King 5:4
Deuteronomy 5:13 – 15	Psalm 62:1

Thank You, Lord, for the new mercies I see today. Everything that I did yesterday or last week, last month or last year, that didn't please You has been removed, washed away and You have thrown all my old stuff into the Sea of Forgetfulness never to drag it up again.

don't have to feel guilty about anything I've done or said. I'm no longer bound to that which created shame in my life. I am no longer tied to the pain. I am released from the misery of my past experiences and able to live in the freedom that comes from being Your child.

Thank you, Lord, for Your forgiveness and not holding me to my past transgressions. Help me to forgive myself as freely as You forgive me.

In Jesus' name I pray. Amen.

Scripture References:
_____
Isaiah 43:25

My heart cried out to You, oh Lord, and in the midst of my sadness, uncertainty and struggle, You answered me from Your holy hill. You saw me and You comforted me. You bowed down to lift me up. You engaged my enemies and You won.

My hope in You is not misplaced. My belief in You is not misplaced. You care for me and have done so all the days of my life. I am assured of Your unfailing love for me and I know my trust in You is not misplaced.

Men may have positions, but it is You who delegate authority. Men may have a say, but it is You who has the last word. Men may plot and scheme against me, but it is Your plan that will never fail. My praise goes to You all day long, for You are my God and King.

In Jesus' name I pray. Amen.

Scripture References:

Samuel 22

Father, as I work to balance my plans for this year, my family, my job or business and my relationship with You, please help me not to fall into the trap of chasing money, fame or fortune; an activity has destroyed many lives.

You know what I need, when I need it and how much I need. Therefore, my hope is in You. You are my provision already met and You are my prosperity. I refuse to make money, fame or fortune my god.

Lord, help me keep my eyes on You. Guard my heart and my spirit from evil. Let me rejoice in You. You are my righteousness. I will continue to praise Your name! In Jesus name I pray. Amen.

Scripture References:

Psalm 97	Exodus 3:13	Exodus 20:3

Father, You will not allow Your righteous ones to be condemned. No matter what is being leveled against us. No matter what men say about us, You, our Lord and Savior, will deliver us out of them all.

I will not fret nor worry. I will seek You and You will deliver me from all my fears. I will call to You and You will answer me. You will save me from all my troubles.

I will lack nothing I need for You, my Lord, will provide everything I need, whenever the need arises. You always provide for Your own. Those who don't believe in You may be in want and lack but never Your children.

Thank You for teaching me to distinguish the difference between Your love for me and what the world calls love. I will praise and glorify You for Your greatness and Your mighty acts that You are issuing on my behalf. I will tell of Your goodness in the land of the living. I pray in Jesus name.

Amen.

Scripture References:

Psalm 34

Father, in the midst of making and fulfilling my plans, please help me to achieve balance in every phase of my life. Help me to be content, but not complacent, with what You have blessed me with thus far in my journey to live a purposed-filled life.

Help me to remain humble while I wait on You. Remind me to cast my cares, burdens, unbelief and lack of trust on You because You care for me.

The world wants me to believe that I have to operate full board every day, all the time. But Father even you rested when Your work was complete. You have created me to have peace of mind, soul and spirit. Help me to find rest in the midst of what can be a maddening pace.

Help me remember I do not have to wear myself out trying to complete my plans. I need to rely on you to be my help. Help me to operate within a balanced lifestyle. In the name of Jesus I pray. Amen.

Scripture References:

Philippians 4:11	John 16:33	Genesis 2:2 – 3
I Peter 5:6 – 7	Mark 6:31	Isaiah 41:13

God, the Father of heaven and earth, show me what I have in my life that I can give to You to help Your people. Lord, help me to see beyond the obvious, to look past what I see with my natural eye that may stop me from giving my best.

Father, I give you all my past hurts and shames that are holding me back. I give You my less than stellar esteem of myself and exchange it for esteeming myself in Christ Jesus. In Christ, there is no condemnation. In Christ, there is no shame. In Christ, my uniqueness is my strong suit for carrying out the tasks You prepared for me before the beginning of mankind.

Savior, help me to know and understand, through Godly wisdom, that I have been ordained by You for service. I have been given my gifts, talents and abilities to be utilized by You to help further the kingdom of God here on earth.

Give me the courage to use my gifts for You. Give me the courage to ignore what people may say and listen to only what You say so I may use my gifts as You have deemed appropriate. Give me Your strength and endurance so I can fulfill Your will for my life.

I believe You will answer my prayer. I thank You in advance for Your faithfulness to Your word over my life. In Jesus name I pray. Amen.

Scripture References:

Deuteronomy 31:6	Romans 8:1	Ephesians 2:10
Psalm 139:16	Romans 12:1 – 21	
Proverb 19:21	I Corinthians 2:9	

Father it seems that one thing after another keeps springing up in my life. Just when I think I can see the light at the end of the tunnel, BAM, all goes black again because another issue has come up. I'm shaking my head! It feels like it will never stop!

On the outside it looks impossible but nothing is impossible for You. On the surface it looks like I'll never make it through all the obstacles that are draining my finances, swallowing up my peace of mind and attacking my joy. I am exhausted just thinking about it all!

That is why I'm bringing all my baggage to You. Father, I need Your help with:

1. _____

2. _____

3. _____

4. _____

5. _____

I know Lord You will work everything out for my good, even the day of payment for the wicked. My hope is in You, therefore I rest in You, my hope of glory! In Jesus name I pray. Amen.

Scripture References:

Psalm 145:18 – 19	Romans 8:28	Matthew 17:20
John 15:7	Matthew 6:5 – 8	
Proverb 16:4	I John 3:21 - 22	

Father, if I think back, take a good look at my life and I am honest with myself, I have no reason to complain. If I take the time to examine where You brought me from and what You've brought me through I see the good You have shown me over the course of my days far out weights the bad.

Thank You!

Even in the bad times You were working to mature and groom me in an effort to prepare me to become the person You created me to be. Today Father, I will not complain about whatever comes my way. Instead of complaining I will thank You for Your goodness and Your mercy, which is new to me every morning.

I will take time to consider Your goodness toward me and I will speak of Your love for me all day long. In Jesus name I pray. Amen.

Scripture References:

| Lamentations 3:39 | Philippians 4:11 – 12 | Hebrews 13:5 |
| Matthew 6:25 – 34 | I Timothy 6:6-8 | |

Father, help me to listen to the voices of the people who love me, care for me and have my best interest at heart. Sometimes their voices get drowned out by the same loud voices that drowned out Your voice and I end up making bad decisions.

Father God, help me to listen to those who are close to me who have Godly wisdom and will speak the truth to me even if it's not what I want to hear.

I know my spouse, significant other; parents; sibling and close friends know me better than anyone else. I should listen to them because they want what is best for me. The loud voices of the world want me to confirm, even if it's not good for me. The voices of the world don't care about me!

Father, help me to hear and listen to the voices of the people You have placed in my life for my betterment. Help me Lord to block out the voices of the world!

I pray with full sincerity in Jesus name. Amen.

Scripture References:

Proverbs 17:17	Proverbs 27:6
Proverbs 18:24	Proverbs 27:10

Father, I know that without faith it is impossible to please You, but doubt often comes in and shakes my faith in You. Before I know it I'm playing the "what if" game. I'm coming up with "Plan B" just in case You don't show up on time or You don't fix the problem the way I think it should be fixed.

I cause myself anxiety, fear or I'm placing the blame on myself or someone else which causes me to be angry, ashamed or feeling guilty. None of this gives me peace, joy or contentment which means it's not from You and it is not how You purposed me to live my life. Forgive me!

In the midst of turmoil I caused because my faith in You waivers, Your faithfulness towards me never waivers. Thank You!

Lord, I need You to not only rebuke the storms that are brewing in my live but to calm the storms of doubt, fear and unbelief that are developing in me. Father, Your word says if I have faith in You, nothing will be impossible for me. Please help my unbelief!

Help me live by my faith in You; not in man, not in the world system, only You. In Jesus name. Amen.

Scripture References:

Psalm 3:5 – 6	Isaiah 26:3	Matthew 6:30
Matthew 17:20	II Corinthians 5:7	Hebrews 11:6
Psalm 118:8	Isaiah 40:27 – 29	
Mark 9:23 - 24	II Timothy 2:13	

Father, today I feel overwhelmed! It's like everything is coming down on me at one time. I can barely breathe! I'm too busy for my own good!

Father, I feel like I moved from having a full plate of things to do, to having an overflowing platter of things I cannot do. I can't even figure out what to do first because everything and everyone is screaming, "ME FIRST!" I feel like my life is spinning out of control. I just want to yell "STOP!" and hit the restart button.

Father I need You to give me an inner calm and an inner peace so I can think. I need You to help me figure out all the stuff I have going on in my life and help me decide what I need to do verses what I can give to someone else to do. Father, help me focus on You so You can focus me.

I know I've done this to myself and I am not ashamed to say I need You to help me sort out this mess. I will do like Jesus; I will pull away from all the stuff and listen for You. I know You will tell me what I need to know. You will give me inner calm and peace. You will help me not to get into this predicament again if I listen and follow You. In Jesus name I pray. Amen.

Scripture References:

Psalm 29:11	Lamentations 3:19 – 26
Psalm 37:7	Matthew 14:23
Isaiah 26:3 - 4	

2 FORGIVENESS

Father, I want to ask for forgiveness. I have not focused on You, Your goodness or the kindness that You have shown me in the land of the living.

I have focused on the things of this world, my financial shortfalls, my hopes and dreams that seem unachievable for me. I've focused on what I don't have much more than I've focused on the good that You provide for me every day of my life. For this, I apologize and ask for Your forgiveness.

Today, I commit to focusing on You and the love and the mercy You have shown me and my family.

In Jesus' name I pray. Amen

Scripture References:

Micah 7:18	Psalms 142:5

Lord, I am blessed because You have forgiven all my sins. You have erased all of my transgressions and You have removed my iniquities, immorality, injustice, wickedness, and sin far from me. You have, for Your own sake, forgotten all that I have done wrong.

Father, why do I hold myself hostage to my past? Why do I continue to judge myself by what I used to be or what I used to do? It's because I haven't forgiven myself. A lack of self-forgiveness leaves me sitting outside the doors of the life You want and have ordained for me to live. Please forgive me for not forgiving myself.

Today, and each day forward, I pledge to hold myself to a different standard. Not the worlds' standards that keeps track of every wrong I've ever committed, but Your standards that give me new mercies every morning so that I may live, breathe and have my being in You.

I submit myself to You, Father; remove the pride, guilt, shame, anger, fear and lack of self-esteem or anything that is in me as a result of harboring what I was or what I've done. I press to move into who You have called me to be for the benefit of Your kingdom.

In Jesus' name I pray. Amen.

Scripture References:

Psalm 32:1 – 2	I John 4:18	Lamentations 3:22-23
Psalm 37:8	Isaiah 43:25	Philippians 3:12 – 14
Psalm 78:38	Isaiah 66:2	

Father God, Your Word says we reap what we sow; today I want to sow only those things that I want to reap.

Please help me make my words kind and gracious, because I want to reap kind and gracious words in my life. Help me to be honest and truthful in all things, because I want honesty and truth in every area of my life. Help me to tame my tongue and my ego, so that everyone I talk to can see the love of Christ in my life. Then Lord, let me reap the love of Christ into my life from You and others.

Let my actions to others be pure so that the actions that others pour into my life are pure. Let my yes be yes and my no be no, so that I don't reap deception. In general, Father, I'm asking You to help me follow the golden rule today: to do unto others as I would have others do unto me.

In Jesus' name I pray. Amen.

Scripture References:

Galatians 6:7	Matthew 5:37	Luke 6:31
Proverbs 20:11	Proverbs	James 3:7-9
Ecclesiastes 10:12	16:13	I Timothy 1:14

Father, forgive me. I know my body is the temple of God. I know my body is the only vehicle You've given me to get through this life. I ask for Your help to take control of my time, Lord. I want a balanced life so that I'm not driven by outside forces to overwhelm myself with things and duties that aren't my responsibility.

Lord too often I let the cares of the world stop me from taking care of myself. I don't exercise the way I should, because I spend too much time working or taking care of things that someone else wants me to do. I don't drink enough water, because I give in to my body's craving for something sweet. I don't eat the food that I should, because I want something fast and convenient.

It's not that I don't have the time; it's that I don't take the time to take care of myself. I allow the pressures of outside forces to run my life instead of taking control.

Help me set the right priorities and say "no" to things that are truly not my responsibility. Help me, Father, to encourage other people to grow by not doing for them what they can do for themselves. Help me to see what You sent me to do versus what I just want to do. Free me from the bondage of too much "stuff" and liberate me from being over-burdened.

In Jesus' name I pray. Amen.

Scripture References:

I Corinthians 6:19	Ephesians 5:29
Mark 4:19	Matthew 11:29

Father, when I look at my life, I know I have no reason to complain. When I think of where you brought me from and consider where I am today, I have no reason to complain.

When I stop for a moment and ponder where You could have (allowed me to go??) taken me and then look at where I am, I have no reason to complain.

I ask for Your forgiveness for whining and complaining when things don't go my way. When it seems that all that I want won't ever be mine, I throw a tantrum like a spoiled brat. Forgive me, because every day You bless me. Every day You keep me. Every day You make provisions for me. Every day You protect me.

So today I purpose not to complain, but to praise Your name for Your goodness and Your mercy.

In Jesus' name I pray. Amen.

Scripture References:

Ephesians 4:29	I Peter 4:9	Isaiah 59:1 – 2
I Thessalonians 5:18	Philippians 4:11 – 12	James 1:2 – 4

Father God, You alone are God! There is no other god besides You. You alone created the heavens and the earth. You alone called forth light and separated light from darkness. You parted the water of the sky from the water of the earth. No one could have done these mighty acts except You!

You, Lord God, brought everything into being that have or had life. You are the only one who calls forth both destruction and deliverance and they must respond to Your call. There is not another God (god, see above) on earth, in the heavens or under the earth. You alone are God!

We, Your children, have allowed the world system to teach us to set up things in the earthly realm as our idols. Things made of clay, steel, plastic and wood. Things such as houses, home fixtures, clothes, cars, jobs, credit and money have become idols.

People such as our children, our spouses, our parents, our church leaders and our supervisors have become idols to some of us. We are more concerned about getting their approval than we are concerned about obeying Your Word.

Some of us have set up intangible things as idols; earthly power, authority and fame. We can't see or touch these things, but we think we know them when we see them.

Forgive us! It was not our intent to place another god before you. Deliver us from the evil of this world and cleanse our hearts. In Jesus name. Amen.

Scripture References:

Genesis 1	Psalm 71:16	Isaiah 40:12 - 26
Deuteronomy 3:24	Psalm 18	

Father, today I acknowledge Your peace that covers and rests on me. Your peace, which is full, complete and lacks nothing, is the peace I need to sustain me. The things the world calls peace; money, wealth, fame and power are fleeting and fad away in the midst of adversity.

Unlike the world's peace, Your peace is always with me, even to the end of time. Your peace is not circumstantial. Your peace is a part of my benefits package of being Your child.

Forgive me for not walking in your peace as often or completely as I should. I allow circumstances and problems to cause me to worry, fret and be anxious. I asked that You help me as I purpose to walk in Your peace every day of my life.

Today I will not worry, fret or be anxious. I will rest in the truth of Your amazing love grace and peace. I pray in Jesus name. Amen.

Scripture References:

Numbers 6:22 – 26	Psalm 29:11	Philippians 4:6 – 7
I Peter 5:7	John 14:27	Proverb 12:25

Father God, forgive us for being multi-faced. Too often when we, Your children, are with one group of people, who believe something that is against Your Word, we say we agree with them. Then, when we're with another group, we say we agree with them. Yet when we're at our houses of worship, we say we agree with Your word even though none of the groups are saying the same thing.

Sometimes we get to the point we feel almost spiritually schizophrenic because we refuse to stand on the truth of Your word. We operate with the weight of lies on our tongues and with deceit in our hearts but still say we are Your children; a royal priesthood selected by You for Your service. Forgive us!

Lord, forgive us for being double minded. We say one thing with our mouths but believe something else in our hearts.

We say You are the author of our faith and then we turn around and come up with our own plan without consulting You and waiting for You to answer.

Father, forgive us for quoting Your word but then being too fearful to follow Your word. Your word says the power of life and death is in our tongues. We keep speaking death over our lives and then we can't figure out why we are spiritually, mentally, emotionally, financially and physically dying.

Our Lord and our God, we need a spiritual refreshing; a heart revival. Please Lord, revive us again! Lord we need You! In Jesus name we pray. Amen!

Scripture References:

Psalm 62:8	Jeremiah 24:7	James 1:6 – 8
Proverb 18:21	Matthew 12:34 – 35	I Peter 2:9
Proverb 23:7	Matthew 15:18 – 19	

Father God, please forgive me for not being diligent and working on the assignments You have placed in my life.

Lord, You have set me free from the law of sin and death, and yet I choose to live as if I was still bound to the dead things of this world. You have freed me to walk in the fullness of Your word, and yet I'm content watching the foolishness of the world on TV and the internet rather than chasing after You.

Help me walk in the freedom that Jesus won for me. Free my mind and my spirit to have a fuller relationship with You through Christ Jesus. Free my mind and spirit to please You rather than man. Free my mind and spirit from being concerned about the world's view. Free me to be single focused on Your view.

Father, help me walk in the freedom that comes from knowing that all my sins are forgiven. There is no guilt or shame that can control me unless I decide to remain bound to my sins that You've forgiven me for committing. I have been set free by the Son of God; therefore, now and forever more, I am free! In Jesus name I pray, amen.

Scripture References:

Proverb 10:4	Galatians 1:10	Proverb 6:6-9
I Chronicles 4:10	I Timothy 4:14 – 16	John 8:36
Romans 8:1 – 3		

Father, I want to ask for forgiveness. I have not focused on You, Your goodness or the kindness that You have shown me in the land of the living.

I have focused on the things of this world, my financial shortfalls and hopes and dreams that seem unachievable for me. I've focused on what I don't have much more than I've focused on the good that You provide for me every day of my life. For this, I apologize and ask for Your forgiveness.

Today, I commit to focusing on You and the love, grace and mercy You show me and my family every day.

In Jesus' name I pray. Amen

Scripture References:

Micah 7:18	Psalms 142:5

3 CHANGE

Father God, I pray the part of the Lord's Prayer that says, "Your will be done, on Earth as it is in Heaven" often without thinking about it, but today I am asking for Your will to be done in my life.

Father, You know what good, right is and perfect for me, because every good and perfect gift comes from You. You know exactly what I need and when I need it. You know how to show Your strength, power and righteousness throughout my life. Today I commit to submit to Your overarching authority in my life. I permit You to have Your perfect way in me.

Lord, when my flesh starts to scream because it is uncomfortable, comfort me by your Holy Spirit. I've been praying for.

(Fill in whatever you've been praying for. Some examples: a closer walk with God, a healthier lifestyle, a mate, a change of heart in your children, a financial blessing, deliverance from past pains, etc.) I know the first step to moving forward is for Your will to be done in my life.

I will not listen to unwise council. I will keep my eyes steadfast and fixed on You because You are the author, the perfecter and the finisher of my faith.

In Jesus' name I pray. Amen.

Scripture References:

Matthew 6:10	I Peter 5:10	Romans 12:1 – 2
Proverbs 15:21 – 23	James 2:23	II Corinthians 1:2 – 4
Matthew 7:11	Hebrews 12:2	

Lord, You are more beautiful than diamonds and nothing I desire compares to You.

Your love for me is more than I can comprehend. Your mercy and Your care for me is from everlasting to everlasting. Your concern for me and my well-being is more than I can fully understand. Nothing I desire compares to You.

My confidence in my work, life and future isn't because of my competence; it is because of Your complete competence that flows through me. I thank You because nothing I desire in this world compares to the surpassing love and greatness that You have shown to me throughout my life. So today, Lord, I only desire Your will for my life.

In Jesus' name I pray. Amen.

Scripture References:

| Psalms 50:1 – 2 | Peter 5:7 | I Peter 2:15 |
| Psalms 136:2 | Corinthians 3:4 – 5 | |

Father, Your Word says that the love of money is the root of all evil. But Your Word also says that money answers all things. You also said that if I seek first the Kingdom of Heaven all other things would be added to me. So Father, this implies that my hope should be in You and You know that I need money as a means of covering my living expenses here on Earth.

You have given me strength to make wealth. That's why Your word says that You will bless the works of my hands and that I will be a lender and not a borrower. You have purposed that I am financially sound and not in debt. The Bible says that You don't want me to owe any man anything except to love him.

Father, with the economy being what it is; so many people are struggling financially. Send jobs to the jobless in our country. Send jobs to the millions of men and women who want to work but can't find a job, so that they can make wealth and pay their bills and not owe anyone anything but love.

Lord, I commit my finances to You. You promised that I'd be the head and not the tail, the first and not the last. Let me be the lender and not the borrower. I commit the works of my hands to You. Bless me, my family and friends to move out of indebtedness and into overflow and abundance.

In Jesus' name I pray. Amen.

Scripture References:

I Timothy 6:10	Matthew 6:33	Deuteronomy 8:18
Ecclesiastes 2:24	Romans 13:8	Deuteronomy 28:8
Ecclesiastes 10:19	Psalms 33:17 – 19	Deuteronomy 28:12
Deuteronomy 28:13	Proverbs 3:9 – 11	

Lord, I know that impossible situations are Your specialty. It is at seemingly impossible and difficult times, when things look bleakest, that You show up and change the course of everything.

Father, in our lives and in the life of our country we have some situations that look hopeless, but by faith we turn to You and find hope:

Hope for family businesses that seem to be dying – restore

Hope for marriages that seem destined for divorce court – renew

Hope for children who have given up on getting an education – revive the dream

Hope for families that have been separated because of job situations – reunite

Hope for finances that have disappeared in our current economic climate – regenerate

Hope for our country's leaders to work together for the good of the common man – revive in our leaders a compassion for all mankind, not just their kind.

In Jesus' name I pray. Amen.

Scripture References:

Psalm 33:18	Psalm 39:7
Micah 7:7	Psalm 37:9
Psalm 33:22	Isaiah 40:30-31
2 Thessalonians 2:16-17	

Father God, it is said that doing the same thing over and over again, expecting a different outcome, is the definition of insanity. I'm tired of acting like I'm insane! I have embarked on a journey of doing things differently and have made a decision to change and pursue a different course.

I am met with obstacles, distractions and deterrents that block my new way of thinking, acting and doing. I find myself wanting to fall back into the old patterns of doing things. When I want to press forward, procrastination is waiting at the door to hold me back. When I want to move into a new area, fear is lurking around the corner. When I want to believe that everything is going to turn out for my best, doubt begins to override my faith. Father, I need Your help.

The old me, the one I wanted so desperately to leave behind, has started creeping into my new journey. I see it, know it, and on some level I feel helpless to do anything to stop it. Then I remember Your word says I will see Your goodness in my life while I am alive. Your goodness, Lord, will set me apart. Your goodness, Father, will help regulate my thoughts and it will cause my heart to be glad. It will allow me to see Your goodness in my life even in the midst of fear, doubt and uncertainty.

Father, I know change takes time and diligence, but I have made a decisive dedication of all that I am to become and all that You have ordained me to be. I am willing to work hard to allow the necessary changes in my thought life, my actions and my attitudes to take place. And while I wait Lord, I will bless Your name.

In the name of Jesus I pray. Amen.

Scripture References:

Romans 7   Psalm 27

Excerpted from the book It's Still Relative, the Word of God for Today's World, pages 81 and 82*

Lord, please help me to see my gifts, talents and abilities as You see them. Father, help me to lean on You – the author, perfecter and finisher of my faith – and not on my own understanding. Help me, Father, to understand the great power You placed in me at the time I accepted You. The power that allows me to be self-sufficient in Christ's sufficiency that abides in me.

Lord, renew my mind so that I understand that there is nothing too difficult for You to perform through me if I yield all my members to you. You are my strength and my shield. Thank you, Lord!

In Jesus' name I pray. Amen.

Scripture References:

Romans 12:6 (Amp)   Proverbs 3:5 – 8

*Used with author's permission.

Father God, when I started this year, I asked for change in my life. I asked to move out of my yesterday and into a new start in You. I asked that Your will be done in my life and that I be released from my old way of doing things, as well as my old thought processes.

Father I can see some change, but there is still too much old junk hovering in my mind and in my heart. I want my life to change so that I can see the newness of You in everything I do. I want to let go of everything that brings me pain, emotional discomfort or an unhealthy lifestyle.

Father, I want a new me in You.

I want to achieve the greatness You purposed for me – and I

will do it.

In Jesus' name I pray. Amen.

Scripture References:

Isaiah 42:9	Matthew 19:26	I Corinthians 15:57
Isaiah 43:19	Ephesians 4:15	Philippines 4:13

Father, when life has beaten me down I often feel like there's no way to move forward, but I also don't want to stay where I am. At those times, I remember one thing: You are my glory and the lifter of my head. When life seems unfair and the pressures of undue burdens fall upon my shoulders, I remember that You are my very present help in the time of trouble. When tears fill my eyes and I want to give up and throw in the towel, I remember Jesus' nail-scarred hands.

There are so many things I could be anxious, upset or worried about, but when I think about (Philippians 4:6). I know that everything is going to be all right and that it's all working together for my good. Lord, thank You for calming the storms in me.

In Jesus' name I pray. Amen.

Scripture References:

Psalms 3:3	Philippians 4:6
Psalms 46:1	Romans 8:28

Father God, what a blessing it is to come before You today and make my request known to You. Today, Father, I want to be like Balaam when he said, "'I must speak only what God puts in my mouth.'"

Lord, set a guard over my mouth. Allow my words to be a fountain of wisdom, not a babbling brook. Let my words refresh and revive those around me, not anger and confuse them. Most of all, allow my words to be few but true. Let no falsehood linger on my lips. May all I do and say bring glory – not shame – to Your name today.

In Jesus' name I pray. Amen.

Scripture References:

Philippians 4:6	Psalms 141:3
Numbers 22:38	Proverbs 10:11

Father, everyday has its own set of challenges. Couple those challenges with my determination to live my life above mediocrity, above the mundane and above the ordinary. I find that trials stand everywhere I turn, waiting to derail my plans. But I won't allow them to do that, because I have the power and the authority of Your Word and the Holy Spirit.

I have been designed to live with purpose and I will not be dissuaded by adversity. I have been designed to live above the law of sin and death; You will allow neither physical sin nor spiritual death to overtake me. I will live to the fullest, because an abundance life has been given to me through Christ.

Today, I take my stand and set my mind on things above and not on things below. I will not be moved, distracted or dismayed. I have been given a victorious life.

In Jesus' name, I am thankful and say, amen.

Scripture References:

| Matthew 28:18 | Colossians 3:1 – 3 |
| John 10:10 | Psalms 20:6 |

Lord God, in the midst of my preparing for great things, help me not to lose sight of You and the work You have already begun in me. Through difficulties, heartaches and circumstances that I had no control over, You began breaking and molding me into the creation You purposed me to be from the foundation of the earth. This breaking process required me to begin some changes that should be carried on for the rest of my life, so You can continue to build on them.

Lord, help me to assess all that I am; all my gifts, talents and abilities should be taken into account. Everything I can do, not just what I like to do, should be considered as possible avenues of improving my overall well-being.

I need to be hones t with myself regarding my shortfalls and the areas where I have below-par performance. Just because I can do something, or I like to do something, doesn't mean it's what I should do.

Father, this type of in-depth look at who I am from the inside out is difficult, sometimes hurtful, and requires a level of truthfulness I am not accustomed to operating in – particularly not with myself. In order for me to correctly judge myself, I need Your Word as a measuring rod. I need Your Word as a guide. I need Your Word as the standard for which I am striving to live. To truly prepare myself for blessings, changes and enrichments, I need Your Word to be a lamp unto my feet and a light unto my path.

Lord, help me. In Jesus' name I pray. Amen.

Scripture References:

I Corinthians 11:31-32   Psalms 119:105

Father, I have so many plans. I have some plans that seem so easy I can carry them out on my own. I have some plans that cause me to stop and say, "Can I really do this?" With You Lord God, I can do all things, but only with You. I cannot leave You out of the plans I have whether they seem easy or difficult. You are the one who has the ultimate control over all human activity.

Father, no matter what my plans are, I want You to direct my paths. I want You to get the glory from the execution of the plans. I want other people to know that my victories are because of the grace and mercy You have shown me. I want other people to know that if You made me victorious You'll do the same thing for them because You don't play favorites.

I know You work everything to its proper end. Help me not to become discouraged or dismayed while I wait on You to work everything out for my good. Help me remember You didn't promise to work everything out the way I want it, You promised to work everything out for my good.

Father God, I commit my plans to You today. I pray in Jesus name. Amen.

Scripture References:

Proverbs 16:1 – 4	Psalm 27:14
Philippians 4:13	Romans 8:28

Heavenly Father, today I will speak Your word over my life. I will not allow my internal enemies – fear, doubt, low esteem, unreasonable concern, hatred, envy or jealousy to cause my words to be anything except gracious, kind, and filled with love and compassionate. This may mean that my words are few today but, if that's what it takes to exhibit Your character to others, so be it.

According to Your word, the tongue has the power of life and death. I choose to live a good life therefore I will speak well of my life. I will choose my words wisely and I say what I want, verses what I don't want, to manifest in my life.

I know my words have power so I will guard my words by Your grace. Lord, I will purpose not to allow my enemies to triumph over me in this area today. Help me to measure my words and think before I speak. I pray in Jesus name.

Amen!

Scripture References:

Psalm 39:1	Proverb 10:19	Proverb 13:2 - 3
Ecclesiastes 5:2	Proverb 12:14	Proverb 18:21

Father God, You have given Your children everything we need to live a full and productive life. You have given us Godly wisdom. You have given us courage and boldness. You have given us the ability to produce wealth; not only material wealth but spiritual wealth. You have given us the power, the authority and the dominion to rule and rein in the earth.

Father, it is true that You have given us all of these things but, most of us don't live up to the greatness You have bestowed on us. Most of us live from pay check to pay check because we're too afraid to walk by faith and fulfill the destiny You have placed in our hearts and minds. Many of us live sad, depressed and less than productive lives because we're trying to live like the world system says we're supposed to live.

Father, too many of Your children are trying to live down to the level of the world rather than living up to the Kingdom of God. You've called and positioned us to live life to the abundant, yet we wallow in the muck and mire of the world. Forgive us!

Father we need Your help to climb out of the pitfalls of this world. Father, help Your children we pray in Jesus name.

Amen.

Scripture References:

Genesis 1:26	Proverbs 22:5 II	Psalm 40:2
Proverbs 3:13	Peter 1:2 – 4	Ecclesiastes 3:11
Colossians 1:12 – 14	Psalm 9:15	Psalm 138:3
Deuteronomy 8:18	Ecclesiastes 2:26	Isaiah 11:1 – 3

Father it feels like I come to You every day looking for something, asking for something or expecting something from You. Starting today, before I ask You for anything or expect anything from You, I'm going to thank You for what You've done for me. I'm going to tell You how grateful I am that You've treated me better than I deserve.

I thank You for forgiving me all my sins. I thank You for not holding the frailty of my humanity against me. I thank You for Your patience and for loving me even when I wasn't loveable. Thank You for blessing me and making me a blessing to others. Thank You for looking beyond my faults and responding to my needs.

Thank You Lord for giving me chance after chance to get my life in Christ right. Thank You God for Your love, grace and mercy that covers the multitude of my sins, both known and unknown. Thank You for loving me back to wholeness in You. In Jesus name. Amen.

Scripture References:

Genesis 12:1 – 3	Hebrews 4:16	Luke 6:37
Ephesians 1:7	Psalm 32:1	I John 1:9
Psalm 19:12	I Peter 4:8	

Father as I change and allow You to change me, I see some of my friends and family members falling away from me. Sometimes this reality makes me sad, angry and somewhat bitter. There are times I think about going back to my old ways but then I realize, that would put my friendship with You in jeopardy.

You are my friend that sticks closer to me than a sibling. You are my only friend who laid down His life for me. The very least I can do is obey You in response for all You've done for me. You are my friend because of Your great love for me, not because of anything I've ever done or anything I can do for You.

You care about our friendship because You created me in Your image. Your friendship is important to me because life can be hard and cruel. I need someone to whom I can turn and in whom I can put my trust.

Thank you Lord for Your friendship, Your love, Your compassion, Your grace and Your mercy to me. In Jesus name. Amen.

Scripture References:

Genesis 1:26 – 27	Psalm 20:7	Proverb 18:24
John 15:13 – 14	James 4:4	Isaiah 41:8 – 10

Father, everyday Your children have a spiritual choice to make; whether we're going to operate with Your bookends of grace and mercy or, if we're going to operate with Satan's bookends of fear and doubt.

Your bookends hold together Your Word, Your promises, faith, love and hope in our lives. Satan's bookends hold despair, depression, hopelessness, anger and anxiety for our lives. The choice of what bookends we want in our lives is ours, individually, to make.

Lord, help us as we make the wise choice to live under Your blessings and evict fear and doubt out of our hearts, minds and spirits by utilizing Your Word of truth just as Jesus did on the Mount of Temptation.

Father, help us as we accept everything that comes with living under Your blessings for our lives. We pray in Jesus name. Amen.

Scripture References:

Deuteronomy 11:26 – 28   Matthew 4:1 – 11

4 SPIRITUAL GROWTH

Father, today I need to encourage myself with Your Word. That's why I say:

I am a child of the Most High God. He will keep me in perfect peace if I keep my mind steadfast on Him, because I trust in Him.

You are my awesome God. No one else has measured the waters in the hollow of His hand or marked out the heavens by the span of His hand. Only You can call the stars out one by one by name and make sure none of them are lost. You are the God that cares for me.

You are the everlasting God. You never sleep nor do You slumber and You never grow tired or weary. You strengthen me because my hope is in You.

When I pass through situations of life that want to overwhelm me, I will not fear because I know You are with me.

When I have to walk into circumstances that cause me heartache and hardship, I will trust in You Lord to bring me out. I will not be afraid, for You will never forsake me.

In the day of trouble, You will keep me safe because You are my light and my salvation—whom shall I fear? Lord, You are the stronghold of my life, of whom should I be afraid?

In the midst of it all Lord, I will praise You. In Jesus' name I pray. Amen.

Scripture References:

| Isaiah 26:3 | Psalms 23 | Psalm 27:5, 1 – 2 |
| Isaiah 40: 12, 26 | Isaiah 43:2—5 | |

Lord, You said, "As a man thinks so is he." So today, I think I am greater than any adversity that may come against me, because greater is He that is within me than he that is in the world. I think I am more than a conquer through Jesus Christ my Lord. I think You are able to do exceedingly and abundantly more than I can ever ask, think or even imagine. I think that You are my hope, song, joy, and contentment in the middle of my battles.

I think that I am the head and not the tail, the first and not the last. I think You will perfect everything that concerns me. I think that I have been made to prosper spiritually, mentally, physically, emotionally, and financially in this life. I don't have to wait until I get to heaven to live a life full of promise, hope and goodwill. I believe that You have purposed that I will live a life full and abundant with everything I need according to Your riches in glory right now.

I think that my family is blessed. I think that the works of my hands are blessed. I think that I am blessed and that I operate in wisdom, power and authority. As I think so I am, therefore I will think upon Your Word and I will be blessed.

In Jesus' name I pray. Amen.

Scripture References:

Proverbs 23:7 (KJV)	Roman 9:22 - 24	Psalms 118:14
III John 2	Ephesians 3:20	Deuteronomy 28:13
I John 4:4	I Chronicles 13:14	Deuteronomy 28:8
John 10:10	I Samuel 17:47	
Romans 8:37	Job 36:11	

Father God, You alone are God and there is no other god beside You.

You alone created the heavens and the Earth. You alone called forth light and separated it from darkness, as well as parted the waters of the sky from the waters of the earth.

You brought everything into being that has or had life and You alone are the one who calls forth both destruction and deliverance. There is not another god on Earth, in Heaven or under the Earth. Anything else we set up as gods are merely idols made of clay and wood.

Forgive me Lord if I've made anything an idol in my life. My spouse, money, car, power, title, position, prestige, fame - or anything else - is not my god. You are my God, my Lord and my Master.

It is not my intent to place another god before You. Deliver me from the evil of this world and cleanse my heart.

In Jesus' name I pray. Amen.

Scripture References:

Isaiah 45

Father God,

Today I know I dwell in the secret place of You, the Highest God, and I am stable and fixed under the shadow of the Almighty, no foe can get to me. I am safe under the pinions of Your wings. I am in the very folds of Your garment and You are my fortress that no one can withstand.

I hear the enemy trying to attack. I hear the enemy calling to me while I'm of my hiding place in You. I hear the words the world system, my flesh and my eternal enemies are saying to me and against me, but no weapon formed against me will prosper and every tongue that rises up against me will be shown to be in the wrong. This is my vindication as a child of the Most High God.

Peace and joy live in my house and in my heart. I know that I have not only overcome the world, but I have conquered the world system through my relationship with Jesus Christ. This world system and all its flaws cannot hold me bound.

I have been made to prosper and be in good health even as my soul does prosper. Through Jesus Christ there is nothing that is impossible for me to accomplish.

In Jesus' name I pray. Amen.

Scripture References:

Psalms 91:1	III John 2	Isaiah 54:17
I John 4:4	Psalms 32:7	Isaiah 55:12
Psalms 94:4	Matthew 19:26	

Father, I will listen for Your voice today. I hear the voice of the world. The voice of the world says, "Despair is the right way. Look at the economy, look at your family and look at your finances. You'll never make it. You might as well give up." But then I hear Your voice say, "I am with you always, even until the end of time. I am your present help in the time of trouble."

I hear the voice of my past reminding me of all the times I messed up. It tells me I'm the same person and that I'm going to mess up now. But then I read Your Word that says I am a new creation. Old things have passed away and everything has become new.

I hear the voice of reason speaking clearly and rationally. "Look at the real world" the voice of reason says, "you have no reason to hope for better. Just do the best with what you have." But then I remember You said that You came to give me life and to give it to me more abundantly and to the full.

Today Lord, I choose to hear Your voice over all the others. Not only will I hear Your voice, but I will believe what You say and ignore the voice of the world and the voice of my past. I choose to listen, obey and follow You today.

In Jesus' name I pray. Amen.

Scripture References:

Hebrews 4:7	John 10:10	Ecclesiastes 8:5
Isaiah 43:25	Psalms 46:1	
Matthew 28:20	II Corinthians 5:17	

Oh, how precious is Your name Lord in all the earth!

You are my family's peace. You are Jehovah-Shalom. You are our peace that transcends all understanding, which garrisons and mounts guard over our hearts and minds in Christ Jesus. You make everything work together for our good because we love You and have been called according to Your purpose and Your will.

I call forth that which is not as though it were and say, "My family is whole. My marriage is whole. My children are whole. My finances are whole. We are whole in every way."

Your peace makes use whole. There is nothing missing or broken in our lives today.

In Jesus' name I pray. Amen.

Scripture References:

Philippians 4:7   Romans 8:28   Hebrews 4:16 – 17

Good morning Father God! As I read Your word this morning I realized that David was in a place of exile from the temple of Jerusalem. He wanted to return to the temple because in his time, the temple housed the Ark of the Covenant, which was a symbol of Your presence with the people of Israel.

In verse 3 of Psalm 43, David says, "...send forth Your light and Your truth, let them guide me; let them bring me to Your holy mountain, to the place where You dwell." And just then Lord, it hit me. I don't have to go anywhere to seek You Father, You are always with me!

You dwell in me! I don't have to go to a special place. I am Your special place! You are in me through the indwelling of the Holy Spirit. I have everything I need to guide me; the light of the gospel of Jesus Christ, which is my bible, and Jesus' truth that lives in me by his word and his spirit.

Thank you Lord for placing in me everything I need to lead a victorious life!

Scripture References:

Psalm 42 - 43

Father, there is one promise that You made that I don't like. You promised that in this life, we will have trouble. My life seems to be filled with this promise right now.

The good news is You also told us to take heart, because You, through the finished work of Christ, have overcome the world. This means that if I am in You, and Your word is in me, I have overcome the world, too. Therefore, I am more than a conqueror because of my relationship with God through Christ.

No matter what happens this week, I will be a success because I have overcome the world system. I do not think like the world, because I have the mind of Christ. I do not allow the things of this world to turn my mind away from the knowledge of my success.

This week, I will proclaim my success with my words and with my actions.

In Jesus' name I pray. Amen.

Scripture References:

| John 16:33 | Proverbs 16:3 | I Corinthians 2:16 |
| John 15:7 | I Chronicles 22:13 | |

Father God, help me make good decisions today regarding my finances, my relationships...in fact, help me make good decisions today in every area of my life.

Help me not to fall for the lust of the eyes, but to do what I know is good and right in Your sight. Lord, help me to say no to things that are currently of little or no value to me.

Things that would make me a bad steward of the resources You've given me if I purchased them, or spent my time doing them.

Forgive me, Father, for complaining about not having enough time or enough money, despite not wisely using what You've provided for me. Father, forgive me for asking for more money, more talents, more time, and more ability when, really, I'm not being a good steward of what You've entrusted to me.

Help me, Father, to identify my shortcomings in the area of stewardship and correct them by allowing Your word to work in me.

In Jesus' name I pray. Amen.

Scripture References:

Exodus 28:30	16:33	Matthew 25:14 - 30
Romans 2:13	Acts 4:19	I John 2:16
Proverbs	Ephesians 6:14	

Lord, strengthen my faith in You. I can't do anything without You. I can't function without You. My faith is waning under the heavy loads that I am carrying. Comfort me, Lord!

Father God, in this world with so much going on, there are a lot of reasons for me to be fearful. People killing each other in record numbers, earthquakes, hurricanes, and the on-going threat of manmade disasters is enough to make me want to stay in the house and never come out. But You have not given me the spirit of fear, but a spirit of love, power, and of a sound and self-controlled mind.

I believe that nothing can come against me that will overtake me. Nothing can rise against me that You, my rock and my help in the time of trouble, have not already conquered. Help me! Strengthen my faith in You; for in You is my hope and my redemption.

In Jesus' name. Amen.

Scripture References:

Psalms 4:3	John 16:33	Psalms 23:4
II Timothy 1:7	Psalms 119:76	Habakkuk 1:12
Psalms 94:19	Psalms 18:2	Psalms 27: 1 – 3

God, I thank You for this day and for Your many blessings. Please help me to have the right perspective on things. Life is short and eternity is forever. I want to start each day reviewing my priorities, and set a tentative plan for where I will invest my time and energy, so that I will be sure to do what matters.

Lord, don't let me be complacent and operate in denial, darkness, deception, and error about the things I need to do. Please give me Your priorities for my life. Guide me and direct my every step.

In Jesus' name I pray. Amen.

Scripture References:

Deut. 28:2	Psalms 25:9	Ecc. 3:11
John 16:13	Isaiah 59:1	John 8:44
Proverbs 10:26 – 28	Proverbs 20:24	

Lord, free me today to be obedient to what You ask of me. Free me to walk on the path You have designed for me.

Lord, do not allow fear, doubt, pride or uncertainty to stop me from moving forward in You and for You. Lord, I have nothing in my life that is more important than fulfilling Your designated plan for me.

Father, I know that it is by faith that I will please You. By faith I know You will bless me for working to renew my mind in the things of God. Father do not forsake me.

Rather, put Your word to work to make a change in me. In Jesus' name I pray. Amen

Scripture References:

Romans 6:16	Ezra 3:3	Psalms 23:4
Proverbs 11:2	II Timothy 1:7	Psalms 33:11
Philemon 1:21	Nehemiah 7:2	Hebrews 11:6
Proverbs 16:18	Psalms 20:4	Romans 12:2

Oh Lord, how excellent is Your name in all the Earth. At times when I would have fallen and never risen again, You were there to keep me safe. When I could have lost everything and been left destitute, You sustained me. When my enemies wanted my demise, You lifted up a standard against them.

There is no other God like You. There is no one who loves me like You do. In light of all Your great works and deeds in my life, I want to say thank You.

When the opportunities arose for my children to stray, You kept them on the right path. When I couldn't see my way, You were my guide. When my business or job was threatened, You worked for my good and brought my business forward, allowing my job to flourish. My competition vanished, but You kept me stable.

You provided me with the strength to withstand the storms of life, and You calmed the raging sea around me; but more importantly, You calmed the raging sea in me, allowing me to be at peace during my storms. While other people who were going through the same things were angry, frustrated, disillusioned, worried, and fretful, You were my comfort.

For these and so many other blessings that You have bestowed on my life, I give you praise.

In Jesus' name I pray. Amen.

Scripture References:

Psalms 8:1	Romans 2:28	I Samuel 2:2
Psalms 48:14	Isaiah 59:19	John 16:33
Psalms 57:6	Mark 4:39	Colossians 3:15

Father, today was not promised to me, but through Your wisdom, grace, mercy, purpose, and plan for my life, You saw fit to let me see another day. For this, I say thank You.

Lord God, help me to be purposeful and focused on my tasks today. Help me not to waste the energy You've given me or be unproductive in my time management. Help me to seize every opportunity to display Your great love for mankind in everything I do.

Help me to not walk in selfish ambition, pride or arrogance, but to walk in humility before You and man. Lord, guide me in obedience to Your plan today. Let me not look back and wonder, "what if," nor let me look too far forward saying, "what then." Let me look at today as the blessing You created for me.

In Jesus' name I pray. Amen.

Scripture References:

Deuteronomy 30:16	Proverbs 11:2	Proverbs 27:1
Philippians 2:3	Proverbs 24:29 – 31	Job 42:2
Colossians 3:15	Psalm 139:9 – 11	Matthew 6:34

Father, I will praise You at all times, because Your love endures forever! When I should have been overrun by my enemies, You upheld me with Your mighty right hand.

Lord, when I should have been cut off and cut out of Your blessings, Your goodness, mercy, loving kindness, and unfathomable love for me through Jesus Christ overrode my sins. For that, I am eternally grateful.

This is the day that You have made. I choose to; be glad of heart, rejoice in contentment and thankfulness no matter what this day may bring my way. I know that if you bring me to it, You will see me through it. There is nothing too difficult for me to understand, nothing too hard for me to accomplish. I am convinced that, because You have ordained this day for me, nothing will confront me that is greater than Your Spirit that lives in me.

am so thankful that Your love for me endures forever. I will rejoice.

In Jesus' name I pray. Amen.

Scripture References:

Psalms 118

Lord, Your grace is sufficient to sustain me through my day. There is so much going on sometimes I feel overwhelmed. But then, I think about Your goodness, kindness and mercy; I realize that You will see me through this episode of my life just as You have seen me through so many other episodes and chapters of my life.

When I look at current situations and circumstances in my life I say, "There's no way I'm going to make it." Then I remember what is impossible with man is possible with God, because with God all things are possible. So Father, today I will purpose to cast all my cares upon You because I know that You care for and about me.

You will work out everything for my good. I will not worry or fret anymore. I will just believe in You and Your ability to do more than I can think or even imagine. I will stand and wait. I will see the deliverance of my Lord in the land of the living.

In Jesus' name I pray. Amen.

Scripture References:

Corinthians 12:9	I Peter 5:7	Psalms 42:8
Matthew 19:26	Micah 6:8	Ephesians 3:20
2 Chronicles 6:40-42	Romans 8:28	Chronicles 20:17
Psalms 55:22	Peter 2:10	
Psalms 57:1	John 14:27	

Father, it seems no matter how much I do, there is always more to do. It seems like the more I do for people, the more they want me to do. They don't seem to understand that my platter is already overflowing with what I have going on in my life. Then when I say, "No, I can't do what you want," they get an unrighteous attitude, as if I've wronged them.

Lord, I'm tired of them! Help me not to take on a bad attitude. Help me not to sin because of my anger. Help me to remain firm but loving with everyone.

Father God, Your Word says that a gentle answer turns away wrath. Help me to answer gently, turn away wrath, and still clearly convey what I mean. Help me not to be wishy-washy in my responses and help me to love everyone with the love of Christ.

In Jesus' name I pray. Amen.

Scripture References:

Proverbs 15:1	Peter 3:15	Ephesians 4:26
Psalms 4:4	Matthew 15:37	James 4:2

Father, I KNOW Your children's blessings are on the way. So sure, in fact, that by faith we will praise You in advance. You promised that if we continue to do what is pleasing in Your sight, You will bless us in due season if we faint not.

It doesn't matter what kind of blessing we're waiting for: a financial blessing, a baby, physical or spiritual healing, healing for a marriage or our emotions. All promises have their "yes" and "amen" in Jesus. Therefore, all Your promises are true because You cannot lie nor do You change Your mind.

We are as sure about our blessings as we are that You will never leave us nor forsake us. We are as sure about our blessings as we are that You are our very present help in the time of trouble. We are as sure about our blessings as we are that You are our strong tower, our fortress and our strength.

We know, beyond a shadow of a doubt, that You will continue to bless us so that we may be a blessing to others. We are sure of all these things, because our assurance is in the completed work of Jesus Christ. So we are sure that the blessing we're waiting for is coming. We will wait and be of good courage, knowing that You always answer our prayers in the appointed time.

In Jesus' name I pray. Amen.

Scripture References:

Hebrews 6:15	II Chronicles 19:9	Numbers 23:9
Psalms 46:1	Psalms 144:2	Genesis 12:2
Chronicles 20:20	Act 4:19	I Samuel 15:29
Deuteronomy 31:6	Psalms 18:2	Psalms 75:2

Father, we pray for every person who carries the responsibility of being an employee. We ask that You give each of us wisdom as we interact with our supervisors, co- workers and our colleagues. Help us to recognize our individual strengths. Help our employers to provide each of us with the necessary tools and resources to get our jobs done. Make them sensitive to our needs, both personal and professional.

Help us to manage what is the most important asset of an organization or company—that is, ourselves. Remind us that we are on jobs to do our jobs. Help us to respect and honor our supervisors, and position us to look at them with our heart as well as our eyes. Give us the ability to communicate clearly the ideas and directions that You have given us. Help us to be open to their input in all business matters.

Lord, grant us the wisdom to balance the tangible, strategic and tactical aspects of every decision with the intangible, sensitive and human aspects involved in making them.

Cause us to see our supervisors as people and not just supervisors. Help our supervisors to see us, their workers, not merely as workers, but as co-laborers with them to complete the duties that we have individually and collectedly been assigned.

Help us, Father, to operate in truth. Help us to work with everyone in an upright and honest way. Give us favor so that they treat us the way they would like to be treated if they were in our positions.

We ask, Father, that You grant us joy and enthusiasm concerning our work. By Your Spirit, help us to see the big picture of our organizations, agencies, companies, etc. Give us the ability to understand that the more we put into our work, the more we will get out of it.

Help us, Lord, to control our tongues. Help us to understand that gossip and backbiting are destructive forces which, in the end, will not only negatively affect our organization but, more seriously, destroy us spiritually.

thank You, Father, for sending us good supervisors— qualified men and women to do the jobs that need to be done. You have said that those You call You also anoint, and that those You anoint, You also equip. Thank You for Your anointing to get the job done above and beyond my own strength, abilities, gifts, and talents. Father, I thank you for the Holy Spirit that goes before me in everything I do. Thank You, God, for preparing my way for greatness.

In Jesus' name I pray. Amen.

Scripture References:

2 Chronicles 35:2	Proverbs 29:19	James 3:2
3 John 2	1 Timothy 5:21	Matthew 25:21 1
Peter 2:14	Luke 6:38	Hebrews 13:21
Psalm 45:1	Matthew 25:23	2 Corinthians 1:21
Corinthians 7:4	James 3:17	John 2:27

Father God, today I recognize Your supreme authority over everything in my life. You will set everything in my life in order, if I submit to You.

Submission is so very difficult. I want what I want, when I want it, in the way I want it done. But I know that my plans and Your plans may not be the same, and Your plans always prevail. Help me, Father, not to be resentful or angry when my plans fall by the wayside. Help me to rest in Your unfathomable love for me, knowing that You are working everything together for my good. It may not feel good or look good, but in the long run I know it will be for my good.

Forgive me for trying to manipulate circumstances and people. Honestly, I've tried to manipulate You to get my way. Please, Lord, fulfill Your will for my life and let me walk in Your peace all the days of my life.

In Jesus' name I pray. Amen.

Scripture References:

Job 22:21	Proverbs 16:1	Proverbs 19:21
Romans 8:7	Psalms 52:8	Roman 15:13
Psalms 33:11	Proverbs 16:9	
James 4:7	Isaiah 45:11 - 12	

Father God, help me operate like a true Christian today. Do not allow me to re-crucify Christ before the world with my words, my actions or my deeds. Help me to demonstrate the love of Christ at all times and in all that I do.

Help my words to be kind, even if that means I don't speak. Help my deeds to be with the right motives, even if that means no one else sees what I do. Help my thoughts to be in line with Your Word and Your will for my life, even if Your Word and Your will are not in line with my plans.

Help me to be honest with myself today and to judge myself rightly. Lord, show me my shortfalls so that be Your grace and Your mercy may begin to correct my ways. Help me, Lord, to be a true Christian.

In Jesus' name I pray. Amen.

Scripture References:

Hebrews 6:4 – 6	Galatians 5:6	Romans 2:1
Isaiah 3:9 – 11	Psalms 19:14	

Father God, it seems that no matter how much You give me I always want more, different or better – more money, a better job or a different outcome to a situation. But today Father God, I just want to be thankful. I don't want to ask for anything, I just want to give You thanks for all You've done for me.

The fact I can read this prayer means You gave me sight today, thank You. The fact that I can hear my spouse, children, television, neighbor or the truck going down the street means You gave me hearing today – thank You. I have gas in my car or I have the strength to walk to a bus stop, either way, thank You for the provision to get me where I need to go.

Today, Lord, I want to be grateful and thankful. I don't want to take anything for granted; because it could have been different had You not thought enough of me to give me everything I need to move through my day in victory. Thank You.

In Jesus' name I pray. Amen.

Scripture References:

Colossians 3:15   Colossians 4:2

Good morning, Father. You have made promises to me. You promised never to leave me nor forsake me. You promised to always be there for me.

Your promises say that if I turn over my work to You, my plans will succeed. Today, Lord, I want the success You have planned for me.

The world says success is obtaining wealth and riches, amassing fortunes and eminence. But You say that success is following Your Word and being skilled at what I do. So Father, I ask today that You give me the opportunities to increase my skill level in whatever You put my hands to do.

Lord, bless me to do what You have called me to do today. Help me to remain focused on my purpose today. Help me to work as if I'm working for You and not for man, because I know I will receive my reward from You and not from man. I give You my work today, knowing that You will cause me to succeed in what You have called me to do.

In Jesus' name I pray. Amen

Scripture References:

| Joshua 1:1 -9 | Ecclesiastes 10:10 | Proverbs 16:3 |
| Psalms 20:4 | Colossians 3:23 -24 | |

Father, on days like this, when things seem so cloudy and uncertain, I find comfort and strength in knowing that Your plans for me will prevail over everything else. There is no assault that anyone can level on my character, my finances or my overall well-being that can stop what You have ordained for me.

So I say to my foes, both internal and external foes, "Your plan to bring me harm has failed. I have my victory already in hand, because I know that through Christ I am more than a conqueror. I have already won, because God will fight for me. There is no scheme or plan that you can bring against me that will thwart the plans that God has for me."

Lord, my enemy has won a few battles, but by faith, I say I've already won the war.

In Jesus' name I pray. Amen.

Scripture References:

Proverbs 19:21	Genesis 50:20	Job 42:2
Psalms 139:16	Romans 8:28 – 37	Chronicles 20:15

Father, it seems to get harder the more I try to stay focused on Your promises. It feels almost impossible to stay steadfast in Your ways. Life has taken some difficult turns that I couldn't anticipate, and I've been left feeling lost and frustrated. There seems to be no remedy.

Then, I remember that nothing catches You off guard. Nothing flies beneath Your radar. You are aware of everything that's going to happen: when, where and how. So I come to Your throne room today laying my burdens at Your feet and say, "Here, I don't want them anymore. I've tried everything I know how, and still nothing works. I am casting all my cares upon You, because I know You care for me. I won't pick them up and take them with me. From this day forward, they are Yours to deal with."

In Jesus' name I pray. Amen.

Scripture References:

Psalms 55:22	I Peter 5:7	Matthew 11:28 - 30

Father, in the midst of all that is going on in my life, I want to stop long enough to say thank you. Thank You for being my rock on which I can stand when I'm weak. Thank You for being my shield of protection when the world wants to assail me. Thank You for being my hope when I look at what seems like hopeless situations in my life. Thank You for being my guide in the middle of a pathless world.

Thank You for always being there even when I felt lonely. Thank You for caring about me when I didn't even like who I was. Thank You for watching over my loved ones when I can't be there, or am unable to do anything about what's going on. Thank You for standing in the gap for me when I am too tired to defend myself. Thank You for overlooking my shortcomings and my deficits. Thank You for loving me when I don't feel worthy.

Thank you for being the loving, kind, merciful, gracious God that you are.

In Jesus' name I pray. Amen

Scripture References:

Psalms 136

Father, thank You for the freedom Your Son's blood purchased for me: the freedom to do all that You have called me to do, and the freedom to obtain everything You have for me.

Thank You, Lord, for loving me so much and for counting me among Your children. Thank you for giving me the great gift of eternal life through Your Son's blood, which has released me from sin, shame and guilt. I am free! Your word says, "So if the Son sets you free, you will be free indeed."

Thank you for my freedom! Bless God in the highest! In Jesus' name I pray. Amen.

Scripture References:

John 8:36

Father, today I thank You for ordering my steps. I don't always enjoy the way You direct my path, but I'm thankful. I know that even in the most difficult times, if I've been obedient to Your word and Your will for my life, You always lead and guide me into all truth.

Honestly Father, there are times I feel like I'm walking blind, deaf and dumb. I can't see where You're taking me. I don't hear any familiar sounds around me and it seems that no one is listening to me, as if I weren't talking at all. But, then Lord, when I'm ready to give up and throw in the towel You remind me that You will guide me. You are my light in dark places. You make the rough places smooth and the crooked paths straight.

Lord, as I set out today I will not worry or fret about the unknown. I will trust and know that You have my best interest at heart. Thank You, Father, for being here with me all the time, leading, guiding and protecting me in every situation.

In Jesus' name I pray. Amen.

Scripture References:

| Nehemiah 9:19 | Isaiah 42:16 | Isaiah 40:4 |

Father, in the midst of all that is going on in my place of business, my home, my community, and in my church, please help me to stay focused on You. Help me remember that You are always in control. Nothing can hurt me, harm me or cause me distress if I stay under the protective covering of Your loving arms.

If I purpose to stay in Your Word and hold on to it with all my might, I will never be defeated. Oh, things may not go my way, but I will not be defeated. I may have what are perceived as setbacks, but I will never be defeated and I shall not fail.

There is nothing and no one that can intimidate me and make me doubt myself or You. I am whole, well and complete in You. Others may question my abilities, but I won't – I am completely confident in my abilities and capabilities, because You are absolutely competent. My confidence doesn't lie in me, but rather it lies in what I can accomplish by being obedient to You and holding on to Your Word in my life.

So today, I speak Your word over my life and say I am more than able to face and conquer anything that arises in my life or in the life of my family. I am already victorious through Jesus Christ my Lord. Amen

Scripture References:

Deuteronomy 33:27	II Corinthians 3:5	I John 5:14
Hebrews 13:5 – 6	I Corinthians 2:9	
Psalms 18:32	Psalms 91:1	

Father, in the middle of all that's going on, I sometimes find it hard to muster my faith and believe that everything is going to work together for my good. I know that's what Your Word says, but that's not what I see.

I see my financial situation looking bleak. I see my country's financial security teetering on the brink of disaster. I see children rebelling against parents and parents not caring for their children. I see fathers leaving the family

– mentally, physically, emotionally and/or financially deserting their homes. I see war and the forethought of other wars looming on the horizon. There are times that all of this becomes overwhelming.

But then, Lord, I stop, think and listen to my still, small inner voice. I am reminded of one thing: You will take care of me. There is no situation or circumstance that is too big, too lofty or too difficult for God. Whether it's my personal finances or the finances of our country, You will take care of me.

God, Your Word says that the government is on Jesus' shoulders; I have no reason to fear, be dismayed or alarmed, because I know that You will take care of me. There is no government's plan that can stand against the plan of God – nothing they can design that will hurt me or my family, because God will take care of me.

When it comes to my personal finances, this is a season in which I am learning that God's goodness and provision doesn't rest on the balance of my checking or savings account; it rests on His Word that says He will take care of me.

I believe it in Jesus' name. Amen.

Scripture References:

Psalms 142:3-5	Psalms 37:6 – 8	I Peter 5:7
Psalms 33:1 0 – 11	Nahum 1:7	
Psalms 55:22	Isaiah 9:6	

Lord God, in the midst of preparing for the great things You have in store for me, help me not to lose sight of You and the work You have already begun in me. – Through difficulties, heartaches and circumstances that I had no control over – You began breaking and molding me into the creation You purposed me to be from the foundation of the earth. That breaking process required me to begin some positive changes that should carry on which I will build upon them.

Lord, help me to assess all that I am; all my gifts, talents and abilities should be taken into account. Everything I can do (not just what I like to do) should be considered as a possible avenue of improving my overall well-being.

I need to be honest with myself regarding my shortfalls and the areas where I have below par performance. Just because I can do something, or I like to do something, doesn't mean it's what I should do.

Father, this type of in-depth look at who I am from the inside out is difficult, sometimes hurtful, and requires a level of truth I am not accustomed to being open to in my life. In order for me to correctly judge myself, I need Your Word as a measuring rod. I need Your Word as a guide. I need Your Word as the standard by which I live. To truly prepare myself for of blessings, changes and enrichments, I need Your Word to be a lamp unto my feet and a light unto my path.

Lord, help me. In Jesus' name I pray. Amen.

Scripture References:

I Corinthians 11:31-32   Psalms 119:105

Father, there is a song that says; "There's a blessing in the storm." I believe that, because it is during the storms in my life that I learned how to be still enough to hear Your quiet, soft voice.

It is during these times of disturbance and turbulence in my life, that I realize that You are there for me even in the darkness of my despair and desperation. Lord, it is in the storm that You teach me that even if You don't calm the external forces in my life, You can quiet the storms in me.

You can say "Peace, be still," to my fears, worries and insecurities. You can quiet my disquieted heart and calm my fragile nerves. You are my peace. You are my joy. You are my Father who is always there for me.

pray that Your peace would rest, rule and abide in my heart. I ask that You hold back any further devastation from coming to me and my family. Father, we are counting on You.

Therefore, Lord, today and every day I rest in You. I say thank you in Jesus' name. Amen.

Scripture References:

Galatians 5:22 – 23   Matthew 5:45   Philippians 4:7

Father, there is a song that says; "My faith looks up to thee, thou Lamb of Calvary, Savior divine! Now hear me while I pray, take all my guilt away, O let me from this day be wholly thine!"

Lord, if only I could be wholly Yours! I know my life would be so much easier if I just belonged to You but I belong to my family too and they pull me in so many directions. I belong to my job and it requires my time and effort while I'm at work. I belong to my church, to groups and other organizations that all require my time, talents and abilities.

Father, help me to strengthen my faith in You and in the finished work of Christ Jesus, by reading my Bible more and watching TV less. Help me strengthen my faith in You by letting go of some things that You didn't tell me to do, I just decided to do, and let me use that time to go to Bible study or just spend quiet time with You in prayer and meditation.

Father, the more faith I have in You the more I become wholly Yours. I pray in Jesus name. Amen.

Scripture References:

| Isaiah 26:3 | Romans 10:17 | Hebrews 4:1 – 2 |
| Mark 11:22 | Corinthians 5:7 | James 2:17 – 18 |

Father, I am seeing the changes that I have instituted in my life – things I knew needed to change from last year to this year. These changes were designed to make me a better person, a better parent, a better spouse, and a better child of God.

Give me the strength and the courage to be my authentic self today. Let me not compromise who I am or what I stand for in an effort to "go along to get along."

Let me be willing to stand for the truth, whether it's popular or not. Let me be willing to speak what is right in love, so that others may see that there is another way of thinking.

Let me stand firm with what is true, what is right and what is perfect in Your sight; let it be tattooed on my lips and on my heart, so that I won't be willing to give in to the lies or evil intent of others.

God, when I'm willing to compromise or I'm ready to give up, remind me that it is my responsibility to fulfill Your plan and purpose for my life. You don't change Your plan for my life just because I don't find it convenient. I am accountable for the actions, plans and purposes that You have laid out for me. You predestined me to do Your will. It is my responsibility to stay in line with Your will for my life.

Father, in a world that has so many people willing to do anything to get ahead, today and every day, help me to stand on the morals, ethics and truth that You laid as a foundation for my life.

In Jesus' name I pray. Amen.

Scripture References:

Psalm 46:1 – 3	Philippians 4:8
II Corinthians 6:14	Proverbs 19:21
(Message Bible)	II Thessalonians 2:14 – 15

Father God, You want me to move in excellence in everything
I do in my home, on my job, at my place of worship, and in my
community. You have equipped me to do everything that you have
ordained for me. You have graced me to move in excellence.

I work with diligence and perseverance in everything I do just as if
I was working for You.

Help me remember that I cannot move or work in excellence
in this phase of life without good health. I need a healthy diet,
exercise, enough rest, and regular check-ups to ensure my health is
intact so that I can move through life victoriously.

Please help me look at all the activities that I have on my plate and
remove things that I shouldn't be doing. Help me look at what I do
for my spouse, my children, my co- workers, my supervisor, my
church family, and others with a critical eye. Help me to honestly
assess whether or not what I'm doing is really mine to do, or if I'm
standing in the way of someone else doing his or her job.

Moving in excellence does not mean being all things to all
people. Moving in excellence means being the best me I can be in
everything You have given me in order to fulfill Your plan for my
life.

In Jesus' name I pray. Amen.

Scripture References:

Philippines 1:9 – 10   Ephesians 6:7 – 8
Colossians 3:23 – 24   Titus 2:7 – 8

Father, I watch TV and see that things haven't changed as much as I had hoped. Fear, doubt, hate, war and violence are still the weapon of choice by our eternal enemy. Many times when I'm watching, listening or reading the news I have to remind myself that You have not given me a spirit of fear, but a mind of love, power and self-control.

I have to remind myself that You, the creator of heaven and earth, are my shelter and my hope in the midst of danger.

You are my mighty and impenetrable force and security. You are my well proven, right now help; just as You have been before. You are my ready and reliable God!

When things don't look like they're going to work out in my best interest I have to remind myself that El Elyon, the Most High God, dwells in me and has given me a portion of His divine, dunamis power. You will break the power of my enemy. You have already made me victorious.

So today Lord, I will cease war like activities and rest in my personal knowledge; my past experiences with You. I will rest in the fact that my God is supreme! The Lord of the heavenly host is with me! His divine power is my defense and my cliff which makes me inaccessible to my enemies! Hallelujah! I pray in Jesus name. Amen!

Scripture References:

Psalm 46   Timothy 1:7
Corinthians 15:57

Father God, I thank You for being my friend. I know that You're my friend, because of the finished work of Christ Jesus. I know that Jesus came to close the gap between us that had made me Your enemy, but because of Jesus' birth, death and resurrection, You now count me among Your friends just as You counted Abram as Your friend.

You and I are not peers. You are my Lord and King, and I am Your handiwork. I was fashioned after You, formed in Your image and created to fulfill Your purpose for my life. You are the author of everything; I am Your vehicle for getting it done on the earth.

You are my friend because of Your great love for me, not because of anything I've ever done. You are my friend because You created me to be like You, but not to be You. You're my friend because life can be hard and cruel, and I need someone to whom I can turn and put my trust. Thank You Lord for Your friendship, Your love, Your compassion, Your mercy, and Your grace.

In Jesus name I pray. Amen.

Scripture References:

James 4:4	John 15:13 – 15
James 2:23	Proverbs 18:24

Lord, I thank You for the history I have with You. You have been with me from the beginning and You appointed everything in my life; my birth, and all the circumstances surrounding it, were appointed by You. My life, at every turn, has Your fingerprints on it. There is nothing about me that You don't know.

Please Lord, help me to remember my life was set apart by Your will, and everything that You ordained for me shall come to pass. Help me not to view my hardships, trials or tribulations as permanent, thereby causing me to deal with the problem as a permanent fixture in my life. Help me to view the difficulties I face with Christ-like understanding and Godly wisdom. Help me to remember what You've already done for me.

I know the problems I face will work for my good, because I love You and have been called to Your royal order. Jesus is my Lord and the Most High God is my Father, therefore I have no need to worry nor fear, for Jesus is my very present help in the time of trouble.

Thank You, Lord, for helping me to see with spiritual eyes that I do not have to worry about my life or body, for You have already prepared a plan to take care of my every need. It is a plan to prosper me not to hurt me; You are my hope and my future. Thank You Lord for Your words of assurance and the Your acts of loving kindness.

In Jesus name I pray. Amen.

Scripture References:

Psalms 139:13 – 18	Matthew 6:25 – 34
Romans 8:28 – 29	Jeremiah 29:11

Lord, when it seems that everything is going wrong and nothing is going the way I had planned, I find my strength and my hope in the knowledge that You are the perfect God. Everything You do, everything You purpose and everything that You ordain for my life is perfect.

Nothing can replace the lessons I've learned by going through adversity, all the while knowing that You are my very present help in the time of trouble.

Nothing can help me grow and mature more than the difficulties of everyday life, while still clinging and holding steadfast to Your unchanging hand. Nothing can prepare me for some of the things I have faced or I am facing, but knowing that You are the same God who helped me through other trials and heartaches calms my heart and soothes   my fears.

Father, I'm not saying I enjoy the difficult and uncertain times, but I am saying that I appreciate knowing You're right there with me, to comfort and protect me because You're that kind of friend.

Thank you, faithful God. Amen.

Scripture References:

| Samuel 22:31 – 37 | I Corinthians 12:6 | Deut. 31:6 |
| Psalms 46:1 | Numbers 23:19 | James 2:23 |

Father, I know I'm going to meet challenges, but when I face them I will say, "I am a child of the Most High God. He will keep me in perfect peace if I keep my mind steadfast on God because I trust in Him."

I will tell my problems that my God is the awesome God. No one else has measured the waters in the hollow of theirs hand nor marked out the heavens by the span of their hand. Only my God can call the stars out one by one, call each one by its name and make sure none of them are lost.

I will tell my adversities that my God is the everlasting God. He never grows tired or weary. He strengthens me because my hope is in Him. When I pass through situations of life that want to overwhelm me, I will not fear because I know that God is with me.

When I have to walk into circumstances that cause me heartache and hardship, I will trust You to bring me out. I will not be afraid for You Lord God, will never forsake me.

Father God, I believe and will walk in Your word. In Jesus' name I pray. Amen.

Scripture References:

| Isaiah 26:3 | Psalm 27:5, 1—2 | Isaiah 43:2—5 |
| Isaiah 40:29—31 | Isaiah 40: 12, 26 | |

Father God, today the Spirit of Truth abides in me and teaches me all things. He guides me into all truths.

Therefore, I say I have perfect knowledge in every situation and every circumstance that I come up against because I have the wisdom of God. I will make good decisions and choices today because I will allow my spirit man to guide my physical man. Not the other way around.

I trust in the Lord with all my heart and I lean not unto my own understanding. In all my ways I will acknowledge You and You directs my path. Therefore, Father, I have no reason to fret or worry because my day has been ordained by You. You alone will make this day perfect for me.

In Jesus' name I pray. Amen.

Scripture References:

| John 16:13 | Proverbs 3:5 |
| James 1:5 | Proverbs 3:6 |

You will keep me safe. You are my light and my salvation

—whom shall I fear? You, Lord God, are the stronghold of my life; of whom should I be afraid?

am encouraged because I know You made me the head and not the tail, the first and not the last. I will be blessed when I go into a situation and I'll be blessed when I come out. You are going to bless the works of my hands if I obey Your commandments.

You, the Creator of all things, have not given me a spirit of fear, but of power and of love and of a self-controlled, well- balanced, calm, and sound mind. I will not be seized with alarm, because no one – not in heaven nor on earth – can do anything to me that You don't allow. I am strengthened and fortified by Your Word.

Because of my relationship with You Lord, I have strength for all things through Christ who empowers me. Because my hope is in You, I am ready for all things and equal to anything through Christ who infuses me with inner strength. That is: I am self-sufficient in Christ's sufficiency. So, no matter what the day may throw at me I'm ready, prepared and completely capable of overcoming any obstacle. This is my day!

In Jesus' name I pray. Amen.

Scripture References:

Psalm 27:5, 1—2	Isaiah 54:15—17
Deuteronomy 28:1—14	Philippians 4:13
Timothy 1:7	Philippians 4:5

Father God, sometime people say, "If you're going to pray, don't worry. And if you're going to worry, don't pray." But, truthfully Lord, sometimes in my humanness I worry about the outcome of things that are going on in my life even though I know that in You I am equal to and fit to contend with everything that presents itself to me, whether it's good or bad.

And yes, sometimes I worry and I pray, then I remember that no matter what the day brings You are still God. You watch over me to protect me. Everything that concerns me concerns You. There is nothing that I'm going to deal with, nothing that is going to confront me, that is too big for You to handle.

Worry has to leave when I really think about who You are and who You are to me. Worry has no place in my heart when my faith in You shows up. Father, help increase my faith. Show Yourself strong in every situation or circumstance that I will encounter today.

I pray in Jesus name. Amen.

Scripture References:

| Matthew 6:25 – 34 | Luke 21:14 | Joshua 23:3 |
| Psalm 31:3 | Psalm 109:21 | I Samuel 12:22 |

Lord, I am so thankful that Your peace and favor rest upon me. I am so glad to know that nothing that comes against me today can cause me to fall out of Your divine plan for me or cause me to fail to be Your child. I am the apple of Your eye and the center of Your attention. Nothing can stop me from taking my rightful place as Your most beloved child. I am so grateful!

Knowing You makes my heart merry. You keep my mind strong in the middle of all the stuff that comes to make me stumble. I stand firm on one truth: You are my loving, kind, forgiving, ever-present Father. Family issues may come against me, work woes may arise, economic concerns may assail me, but none of it will steal my joy, which comes from You.

Thank you for being here for me no matter what. In Jesus' name I praise You, Father. Amen.

Scripture References:

Luke 2:14	Psalm 16:9	Roman 8:15
Nehemiah 8:10	Psalm 17:8	

Father, today I put my pride aside and seek after the peace that can only come from You. My heart desires You, my soul requires You and my life is in need of You.

Help me to quiet myself before You and humble my life under Your mighty hand. Help me not to worry nor fret excessively. Neither worry nor fretting can change the outcome of anything going on in my life. Worry and fretting only cause me to worry and fret more.

My hope is in You, Lord God. Nothing or no one else can give me hope.

In Jesus' name I pray. Amen.

Scripture References:

Matthew 6:27   Psalm 131

Thank you, Lord, for giving me one more day in Your presence. Thank You, Lord, for being there for me no matter the situation, circumstance or what's going on. I can always count on You being there for me.

Even when I'm in a deep valley of life, feeling like nothing good is ever going to happen for me, You are there for me. If I'm having a mountain top experience, where everything in my life is going well and I have nothing to complain about, even then, You're there for me to lead me and guide me into all truth.

You are the God who looks out for me no matter what. You are my God and my father and I am Your child. I am happy to humbly say, "Thank You, Lord, for being there for me."

In Jesus' name I pray. Amen.

Scripture References:

Psalm 139:7 – 10

Lord, You supply Your grace to me in abundance, thank You. I never have to worry about Your love or concern for me because I know Your grace covers me. It is by Your grace and Your mercy that I get to see another day.

My day is full of promise and possibility because of Your grace. From morning until night Your grace is given to me for my good. For this, I am thankful.

Bless the name of Jesus! Amen.

Scripture References:

Romans 5:17

Father, the one thing we can't ever recover is time. Once it's gone, it's never to be seen again. Whether it's a minute, an hour or even a second, time is fleeting as it moves by us and into eternity. Today, Lord, I give You my time. Help me to be productive. Help me do the things I need to do and not just focus on the things I want to do. Help me not to be lazy or a sluggard, but enable me to move out and do what You have ordained for me to do today.

Father, my time is a valuable commodity that You have given me to fulfill all the tasks of my day, and then to find sweet sleep at the end of my work. My time is not intended to be wasted or killed. Forgive me for wasting my time and help me to move into a new level of time management.

Help me manage my time by the tasks You give me to complete and not by my lazy tendencies.

In Jesus' name I pray. Amen.

Scripture References:

Proverbs 13:4	Romans 13:11	Ephesians 5:15 – 18
Psalms 39:4 – 5	Proverbs 10:4	I Corinthians 10:31
Proverbs 26:14 – 16	Proverbs 12:14	
Proverbs 3:24	Psalms 90:12	

Good morning Father God. Today is another opportunity for me to get it right. You've given me another opportunity to let You lead my life according to Your plan and will for me. Help me, Father, to focus on what is good, right and worthy of acknowledgement and to keep the negative and evil thoughts and concepts away from my mind and my heart.

Father, today I choose to walk in the light of Jesus all day long and not to burden myself with things that aren't within my control to change. I will not worry or fret because of evil doers, but I will keep my mind on Jesus and allow Him to direct my path.

In Jesus' name I pray. Amen.

Scripture References:

I Peter 2:21	I Peter 1:14 – 16
Matthew 16:24	Philippians 4:8 - 9

Lord, today is filled with unlimited potential because I'm filled with Jesus Christ. Nothing is impossible for me to achieve because nothing is impossible for You.

My goal for today is to be completely obedient to You, completely sold out for You, completely thankful to You, and completely occupied with You, because I am completely filled with Christ Jesus, which makes me one with Christ.

Christ was completely obedient to You, even unto death. He was completely sold out to You, completely thankful to You, completely occupied with You, and completely filled with You, because You and Christ are one.

Just like You and Jesus are one, I am one with Jesus. He is in me and I am in Him; therefore, there is nothing impossible for me! Thank You Lord for making me one with You.

In Jesus' name I pray. Amen!

Scripture References:

| Colossians 2:6 – 7 | Matthew 17:20-21 | John 15:4 – 5 |
| Colossians 2:9 – 10 | Luke 1:37 | John 17:20 – 21 |

Father, today I purpose to be anxious for nothing, but in everything, with thanksgiving and faith, I will rest in Your unfailing love for me.

Lord, in the light of Your love my worries, anxiety, depression, and internal confusion are overrated. When I consider Your goodness, Your mercy and Your unbridled faithfulness to me, frustration, discontent and nervousness seem overrated. Nothing compares to Your love for me.

Even when I sin and fall short of Your glory, Your grace is there to comfort and protect me. Nothing trumps Your love for me. Therefore, I can rest in You. I can rest in the completed work of Christ.

Thank You, Lord, for rest.

Scripture References:

Romans 8:35 - 39

Father, allow my words to be seasoned with Your love and grace today. Do not let my words betray my actions; neither let my actions betray my words. Let my words and my actions walk in harmony today so that everyone I come in contact with knows me to be a truthful and upright person.

Lord, I know Your Word says that everyone will have to give an account on the Day of Judgment for every careless word they have spoken. Father, do not allow my words to be numerous, nor cause them to stir up anger in other people. Help me to temper my responses today so that my words turn away wrath. Let all my words be aptly spoken and help keep my good reputation intact.

Father God, I pray over every meeting, conversation and activity I engage in today. I pray that all my steps be ordered by You, and that my heart and my mind always respond in obedience to Your directions. I pray that I choose the way of righteousness when faced with many options. Today, it is my sincere desire to fulfill Your priorities and not allow my flesh to dictate my actions or attitudes. This day, I do all things to the glory of God and I am fruitful in every good work.

In Jesus' name I pray. Amen.

Scripture References:

Proverbs 15:1	Matthew 12:36
Proverbs 25:10 – 11	Proverbs 10:19

Lord, this morning I want to thank You for the things that I often don't even think about, yet are the very things that You purposed for my life in order to shape and mold me into the person I am today.

Thank You for my first, second and third grade teachers who taught me to read. Without them, I would not be able to hear Your heart every time I read Your word. Thank you for the times I didn't get a good grade on a test. It was Your way of pushing me to extend myself beyond the mediocrity of the world. Forgive me for all the times I pouted because I couldn't go somewhere, or do something other people were doing. I see now that it was Your way of protecting me.

It was in these simple times, with these simple acts of love, that You let me know You were always there: my invisible God, doing great and visible things in my life. Thank You.

Scripture References:

| Romans 2:13 | Romans 12:2 | Thessalonians 5:18 |

Father, I thank you for the people in my life who rub me the wrong way. I call them Sandpaper People because they are rough and difficult to deal with, but I understand they have a very special job. Their job is to rub off my rough edges and bring me to a place of being perfected in You.

Lord, help me bear my Sandpaper People with love and rejoicing, not anger and resentment. Help me not to run from them, but to see them as the blessings they are; without them I can't grow, mature or become what You created me to be for the Kingdom of God.

Dealing with my Sandpaper People is a challenge. They do their job of getting on my nerves, but I realize that they are a part of Your plan to help me reach a new level of faith, knowledge and maturity in You. They are an important component to my being made perfect in You, which is my greatest reward.

Help me today, Father. In Jesus' name I pray. Amen

Scripture References:
_____

Samuel 22:31 – 33   Ephesians 4:12 - 13

Father, it seems that I have allowed outside forces – other people, situations and circumstances – to dictate my attitude, my focus and how I portray myself at work, at home, in public, and even at church. It's time for me to stop allowing my emotions to have the reins of my life. It's time to bring things into correct order.

am a child of the Most High God, which means I have dominion and authority over my environment, not the other way around. I am subservient only to You, Father. Not one person or thing is greater than me. I have self-control; therefore, nothing and no one can dictate neither my attitude nor my altitude. No one can make me act out of character. If I act out of character, it's because I choose to act out of character.

Help me, Father, to stay true to the new me You have called me to become through my relationship with Your son.

In Jesus' name I pray. Amen.

Scripture References:

Genesis 1:26 – 31	Luke 10:19
Proverbs 16:32	Peter 1:5 – 7

"My faith looks up to thee, thou Lamb of Calvary, Savior divine!
Now hear me while I pray, take all my guilt away;

O let me from this day be wholly thine!"

Father, these are words from a hymn that many of us don't sing
any more, but this morning, it is the prayer that is on my heart. In
the midst of all the turmoil, uncertainty, difficulties, and heartaches
we are facing in the land, my faith looks up to You.

When we are constantly hearing about one tragedy after another
and feel helpless to stop the seemingly never ending tide of
discontent in our country, we have one place on which we can
place our faith: the Lamb of Calvary, our Savior divine.

Father God, in the name of Jesus, please help my unbelief. No
matter the situation or the circumstance, I know You're more than
able to make every good and perfect gift abound unto me. Father,
I say a special prayer for those who don't know they can pray and
that You will hear and respond to their prayers.

Father, today, no matter what, my faith looks up to You because
You are my Savior divine.

In Jesus' name I pray. Amen.

Scripture References:

| Job 14:1 | Psalms 27:5 | John 16:33 |
| Psalms 125:2 | Mark 9:24 | I John 5:3 – 5 |

Lord, I thank You for the rejections I've receive in my life. I know that may sound strange, but I have found that rejection is one of the ways You protect me from things and people that would hurt or harm me.

Rejection never feels good to anyone. It hurts to think others don't want you around, or they don't like you just because you're you. The heartbreak of rejection has ruined many lives. I know that when I'm faced with sting of rejection, I can run to Your open and loving arms and find peace, joy, patience, and understanding. I know that rejection is Your way of keeping me out of harm's way.

Father, in a world that rejects anything or anyone that refuses to conform to its ideals and thought patterns, I rejoice in knowing that I've been accepted by You, the Creator of all things. Thank You for Your acceptance of me. Thank You for allowing me to see Your love for me through rejection by others.

In Jesus' name I pray. Amen.

Scripture References:

Job 8:20	Psalm 118:21 – 23	I Peter 2:4 – 5
Psalm 27:9	Psalm 119:118	

Father, it seems that I neglect, overlook or take for granted those who love and care about me the most. It seems I'm always reaching for more, aspiring for greater, pressing for something else or moving so fast that I forget to say, "please," "thank you" or "you're welcome" to the very people who are working to help me move to greater heights.

Lord God, help me to be more conscious of how I treat the people who love me the most.. Help me hold them in high esteem and show them how much I appreciate them. Help me to look beyond my ambitions and see that they, too, want to achieve great things. Help me focus on them today: on their needs, their desires, their hopes and their dreams.

Father, please help me to not be so self-centered and self-absorbed. Help me to consider the needs of others, particularly those who are always here for me, before my own. Help me to place them in their own limelight for Your glory.

In Jesus' name I pray. Amen.

Scripture References:

Leviticus 19:18	Galatians 5:14
Mark 12:33	James 2:8

Lord, some days it seems like life is pressing in on me from every side. Bills are due; meanwhile my job is talking about layoffs or work slowdowns. My house is running amuck and I have no one to turn to for relief.

Every time I turn on the television or the radio there's another country in unrest, another earthquake, another flood, or some kind of disaster that is destroying people's lives. It seems like there isn't any peace anywhere.

But, even in the midst of all the madness, I know I have nothing to fear because You are with me. Your love and Your kindness cover me. I will not be afraid. You are my helper and I have comfort in knowing that, in the end, I will be triumphant over those who try to oppress me.

I will take my refuge in You, Father God, knowing that I can trust You and depend on You to be my strength and my song in the midst of the most difficult times. I can say without hesitation, "I will live – not just survive, but live – and will declare God's goodness, mercy and favor towards me."

In Jesus' name I pray. Amen.

Scripture References:

Psalms 23:4	Psalms 118:6 – 9	Psalms 118:17

"Now faith is **(the certainty)** being sure **(confident, affirmed, resolute, assured of what I know, having the title deed)** of what I know and certain **(the proof of conviction)** of what I do not see **(and the conviction of their reality)**."
Hebrews 11:1 NIV*

Lord, my faith looks up to You. It is in You that I have my assurance, my confidence and my conviction. I will not waiver or shrink in the face of neither my enemy nor my opposition.

For You, Lord God, are my strength and my shield. Your rod and Your staff – Your protection and authority – are mine. Who can stand against You? Who can change Your plan? Who can void Your plans for me? No one and nothing can stand against You or thwart Your plans for me.

I will stay under the pinion of Your wings and am resolute in my confidence in You. My faith is in You; therefore my faith is in Your word, which is the truth. My faith looks up to You. Thank You for being a faithful God.

In Jesus' name I pray. Amen.

Scripture References:

Psalm 23:4	Hebrews 11:1	Proverbs 19:21
Proverbs 21:30	Psalm 33:11	
Psalm 28:7	Psalm 91:4	

*Words in bold type were added by the author for emphasis and under the direction of the Holy Spirit.

You to help Your people. Lord, help me to see beyond the obvious, to look past what I see with my natural eye that may stop me from giving You my best.

Savior, help me to know and understand, through Godly wisdom, that I have been ordained by You for service. I have been given my gifts, talents and abilities to be utilized by You to help further the Kingdom of God here on earth.

Give me the courage to use my gifts for You. Give me the courage to ignore what people may say and listen to only what You say, so I may use my gifts as You have deemed appropriate. Give me Your strength and endurance so that I can fulfill Your will for my life.

I believe You will answer my prayer. I thank You in advance for Your faithfulness to Your Word over my life.

In Jesus' name I pray. Amen.

Scripture References:

I Corinthians 12:1 – 11

Father You are my peace! More than just my peace, You are my Shalom. You are the reason I am complete; nothing missing in of my life, nothing out of place. You are the fulfillment of everything I need, when the need arises. You are the "I Am Who I Am" God.

Father, when everything seems to be going to hell in a handbasket, You lift up a standard again my enemy; a human enemy, a supernatural enemy or my own flesh that doesn't want to submit to my spirit person. You lift up a standard against the enemy that rages in me! You are my Shalom!

Yes Father, I recognize that sometimes I'm my own worst enemy. My old habits, my old thought patterns and my old attitudes want to rise up and have me live the way I use to live before Jesus became my Savior and Lord. Jesus paid too high a price to redeem me back to You Father, for me to allow my old ways to drag me backwards! You are my Shalom!

I am a new creature, old things have died and I am new in Christ Jesus. I have His Shalom living in me! I have Jesus' Shalom quieting my flesh! I will submit to the Shalom of Christ and I will not allow the raging storms in my life to cause me to operate like my old self. I am a new creature and I am full of the Shalom of Christ. I believe and walk in it, in Jesus name. Amen.

Scripture References:

Exodus 3:14	Galatians 4:4 – 9	John 14:27
II Corinthians 5:17	Isaiah 59:19	I Corinthians 9:27
Isaiah 43:18 – 19	(Amplified)	

Father, when I'm faced with difficult situations and circumstances my humanity comes to the surface. I know Your Word says that You haven't given me the spirit of fear but sometimes I am fearful.

Father Almighty, when I am dealing with the illness of a loved one, I feel fearful of losing them. When I faced with the loss of income, I am fearful of losing my home, car or other possessions that I need. When I'm confronted with the loss of a friend because they don't want to hear the truth, I become fearful because my relationship with them is important to me. Forgive me Father, but I'm only human.

I know that as long as I am alive a certain level of fear is going to surface from time to time but, I refuse to allow fear to control my mind or my emotions. That's why I run to You and find shelter in Your Word.

Your Word reminds me that You are Elohim, the creator of heaven and earth; You are the God of everyone and everything! Nothing is greater than You. No illness, no financial shortfall; nothing is greater than You!

When I run to Your Word my fears are relieved because Your reminds me of Your unfailing love and greatness. Thank You for being my fortress, my refuge in difficult times and my very present help in the time of trouble. Thank You!

In Jesus name I pray. Amen.

Scripture References:

| Psalm 46 | John 1:1 – 4, 14 |
| Proverbs 30:5 – 6 | II Timothy 1:7 |

As I read Your word this morning I realized that David was in a place of exile from the temple of Jerusalem. He wanted to return to the temple because in his time, the temple housed the Ark of the Covenant, which was a symbol of Your presence with the people of Israel.

In verse 3 of Psalm 43, David says, "...send forth Your light and Your truth, let them guide me; let them bring me to your holy mountain, to the place where you dwell." And just then Lord, it hit me. I don't have to go anywhere to seek You Father, You are always with me!

You dwell in me! I don't have to go to a special place. I am Your special place! You are in me through the indwelling of the Holy Spirit. I have everything I need to guide me; the light of the gospel of Jesus Christ, which is my bible, and Jesus' truth that lives in me by his word and his spirit.

Thank you Lord for placing in me everything I need to lead a victorious life!

Scripture References:

Psalm 42 - 43

Father God, today I purpose to walk into my full potential in everything with my whole heart. I will not hold back or reserve anything that needs to be expended in order for me to fulfill my appointed course in You today.

cast down excuses, lies deceptions, denials and procrastination. I throw off guilt, shame, laziness and slow- fullness. I run full tilt into that which You have designed for me today. In Jesus name. Amen.

Scripture References:

Ephesians 3:17 – 20	Romans 1:8 – 10	Corinthians 4:2
Psalm 139:16	Proverbs 14:8	Ephesians 4:17 – 25

Father, I watch TV and see that things haven't changed from one year to the next. Fear, doubt and hate, war and violence are still the weapon of choice by our eternal enemy. Many times when I'm watching, listening or reading the news I have to remind myself that You have not given me a spirit of fear, but of a mind of love, power and self-control.

I have to remind myself that You, the Creator of heaven and earth, are my shelter and my hope in the midst of danger.

You are my mighty and impenetrable force and security. You are my well proven help, right now as You have been before; You are my ready and reliable God!

When things don't look like they're going to work out in my best interest I have to remind myself that El Elyon, the Most High God, dwells in me and has given me a portion of His divine, dunamis (miraculous) power. You will break the power of my enemy. You have already made me victorious.

So today Lord, I will cease war like activities and rest in my personal knowledge; my past experiences with You. I will rest in the fact that my God is supreme! The Lord of the heavenly host is with me! His divine power is my defense and my cliff which makes me inaccessible to my enemies! Hallelujah! I pray in Jesus name. Amen!

Scripture References:

| Psalm 46 | Corinthians 15:57 | Timothy 1:7 |

Father, sometimes I feel like I can't go on. I can't get through this round of difficulties. I can't press through this trial. My flesh is crying for everything to end; all the heartache, hardships and difficulties, so I can live what I call a "peaceful life".

But the three Hebrew men had to be delivered from the furnace in order for the king to recognize You as the King of kings. The king had to see the King of kings do the miraculous before he was willing to acknowledge there was a God greater than his gods and a King greater than him.

In this world system there are a lot of kings and gods; our government system, the rich and powerful and corporations to name a few. Sometimes You have to put Your children in the furnace in order to prove to the kings and gods of this world that You are the only true God and sovereign Lord and King.

Thank You for trusting me to go into the furnace. Thank You for giving me enough faith to know You will deliver me unharmed. Thank You for instilling in me enough faith in You to know that You have my best interest at heart and You will never leave me nor forsake me.

Thank You for trust me with suffering for Your glory! I pray in Jesus name. Amen.

Scripture References:

Daniel 3:19 – 27   Hebrews 13:5   Job 42:2

Father, I feel like a fish out of water today. The place where You currently have me is not where I had planned to be. It is uncomfortable and I feel out of place and out of sorts.

There is nothing I can do to change where I am. I didn't bring myself to this place and I can't remove myself from where I am. Only you Father God can move me. I understand that You have positioned me in this place to force me to trust in You and You alone.

I thought I was trusting only in You before but know I realize I wasn't. I was trusting in my marriage, my job, my bank account, my retirement plan, my stock portfolio or any number of other things in the world system. Please forgive me.

I can't lean on or depend on my own understanding because I really don't know what's going on. I want to yell, "why me?" but that won't help. Father, I want You to tell me what I have to do to get out of this situation so I can get back to my "normal" life. But I have learned that You love me too much to rush me through a lesson. The truth is I belong to You. I was purchased with the life of Jesus Christ. You can use me as You see fit because my life is Yours.

You know what is best for me and I know I have to trust that as my truth not just a saying. I have to trust You.

Father, help my unbelief. I pray in Jesus name. Amen.

Scripture References:

| Jeremiah 10:23 | Proverbs 3:5 – 6 | Mark 9:24 |
| Job 32:25 – 29 | Proverbs 20:24 | |

Father waiting for You to answer our prayers can be so hard. Watching the ungodly succeed while Your children struggle and sometimes suffer can be difficult to see. But I know You will answer Your children's cry and meet every one of our needs.

So today Lord, I ask that You strengthen us who are waiting for You to answer our prayers. I pray that You will remind us that our hope is in You. Remind us Lord that You will protect us from anything that rises up against us while we wait for You to meet us at our point of need.

Father, remind us that Your plan for our lives can never be derailed. Just because things aren't going the way we planned doesn't mean things aren't going the way You planned. Your plans for us stand forever while our plans are as fleeting as vapors.

God, remind us that You are dependable and Your word and works stand forever. You are loyal in Your love towards Your children and Your unfailing love surrounds us at all times. Put in the forefront of our minds that Your favor lasts a lifetime. Uphold us while we wait. I pray in Jesus name. Amen.

Scripture References:

| Psalm 17:6 | Psalm 32:10 | Psalm 38:15 |
| Psalm 27:14 | Psalm 33:11 | |

Father God, today I refuse to walk in fear or doubt. I will not lean to my own understanding but I will trust in You. Father, You created me in Your image and in Your likeness. I am perfected in You. I am able to accomplish everything You've planned for me.

have been made righteous in You. My former ways have passed away and in You I have become a new creation. You have made me an ambassador to the lost, the least and the less than; to bring them to reconciliation to You through Jesus Christ Your son.

Lord, sometimes I think I'm not good enough to fulfill Your plan for me. I asked that as I embark on my tasks as Your ambassador, remind me that I am a part of Your royal priest hood. A part of Your holy nation and You are the only one greater than me.

Thank you God for thinking enough of me to call me Your child and making me more than a conquer through Your son Jesus Christ. Help me be an obedient and mature child of the Most High God. Help me to walk out the path You've carved out for me. I pray in Jesus name. Amen

Scripture References:

Proverbs 3:5 – 6	Romans 8:37	Corinthians 5:17 – 20
I Peter 2:9	Hebrews 10:13 – 14	Ephesians 4:23 – 24
Genesis 1:26 – 27	I Peter 1:13 - 16	

Father, there are days I set back and watch evil, mean spirited people prosper while good people struggle. These are the days I wonder what You're doing. Don't You see? Don't You care?

It seem so unfair that people who are mean, hateful, under handed and liars get away with so much while the good people who deserve more don't get what They need. I know the evil people get their pay back in eternity and the good people get their reward in eternity but we live in the here and now.

I know that your plans stand firm forever and the purpose of Your heart is through all generations. I know that the righteous should not get angry, indignant or be envious of evil people but I see their plans prospering while the plans of the righteous languish on the vines of life. I just don't understand! What about the good peoples plans? What about our hopes and dreams?

Even though I see all of these things, I will trust in You and I will do good. I will be thankful for what You've already given me. I will delight myself in You and I will wait while You complete Your plan to give me the desires of my heart. I will wait on You. I pray in Jesus name. Amen.

Scripture References:

Psalm 33:11   Psalm 37:1 - 4

Oh Lord, how excellent is your name in all the earth! When I would have fallen and never risen again, You were there to keep me safe. When I could have lost everything and been left destitute, You sustained me.

When my enemies wanted my demise, You lifted up a standard against them. There is no God like You! There is no one on earth nor in heaven that love me as much as You do. In light of all Your great works in my life I want to stop and say "thank you".

When I couldn't see my way, You were my guide. Thank you!

When my business or my job was threatened You worked it out for my good. Thank you!

When my children were given the opportunity to stray, You kept them on the right path. Thank you!

For these and so many other blessings that You have bestowed on my life, I give you praise. I pray in Jesus name. Amen.

Scripture References:

| Psalm 8:9 | Psalm 34:7 | Psalm 55:16, 22 |
| Psalm 18:4 – 6 | Psalm 50: 14 – 15 | |

Father God, thank you for making me the apple of Your eye. I will walk in the fullness of Your glory and will not fall short of the abundance You have for me.

I am overwhelmed by the fact that there is nothing in my life that does not concern You. Everything; my spiritual, mental, physical, financial and emotional health is all import to You. There is nothing or no one who is more important to You than me.

The light of this truth propels me to walk into the destiny You have designed, purposed and planned for me. Knowing that nothing You have planned for me can be stopped, gives me the courage to pursue what You have purposed for me.

You don't hold my past against me and neither will I. I press forward; leaving yesterday, last month and my earlier years in my rearview mirror. I move forward to what You have for me.

Moving forward in Jesus name! Amen.

Scripture References:

| John 10:1 | III John 2 | Nahum 1:7 |
| Psalm 55:22 | Proverb 21:30 | Deuteronomy 32:10 |

Father, allow Your glory to fill my heart today. Let Your peace prevail in my life. Let Your joy overflow in my home and allow Your grace and mercy to cover every aspect of my life. I feel that things going on in my life are trying to overtake me, but I will open my heart and mind to Your peace, joy, grace and mercy, and I will find rest for my soul.

Everything is not going the way I wanted or expected it to go but I put my trust in You. Even though I don't understand what You are doing, I know You have my best interest at heart and are working to prefect me in Christ Jesus.

I know You have a purpose and a plan for me. I know You have placed me on this path so I can fulfill You plans. I will trust in Your unfailing love for me and will walk on this path until You tell me to do something else. I will trust Your peace, joy, grace and mercy to override all outside factors that are vying for my attention. I will keep my eyes stable and fixed on You. I will trust You to lead me safely on my journey to fulfilling Your plans for me. I pray in Jesus name. Amen.

Scripture References:

Psalm 13:5 – 6	Psalm 37:3- 9	John 14:1
Psalm 20:7	Nahum 1:7	

Good morning Father God! Thank You for this day and the many blessings You have determined to bestow upon me today.

Please help me to have the right perspective on things. Life is short but eternity is forever. I want to work on and walk in the things that are going to follow me into eternity. I don't want the work I do here on earth to have no heavenly gain.

Father I want to start each day with my priorities in place and a tentative plan for where I will invest my time and energy. I want my life's focus to be about what matters to You.

Lord don't let me be complacent and use denial and lies as excuses for not doing what You've purposed for me to do. Please clearly give me Your priorities for this season of my life. Guide and direct my steps so that I may fulfill Your plan and purpose for my life. I pray in Jesus name. Amen.

Scripture References:

Proverbs 14:8	John 16:13
Proverbs 23:23	I Corinthians 9:24

Father, I pray for a spirit of diligence. Too often I start out doing something and then I allow it to fall to the wayside. No matter what it is that I start; a new eating program, an exercise program, spending more time with You, I always starts well but I don't continue in my pursuit.

I get discouraged, frustrated and sometime even bored so I stop doing what I need to do and go back to doing the very things I want to stop doing. Father, forgive me and help me!

Father I know Your word says that the diligent become rich, not just rich in money but rich in our knowledge of You, our character and our ability to withstand obstacles when they come against me while I doing Your will.

I know Your word says that I will get what I want if I don't stop doing what is right and I continue to press forward. I also know that a sluggard, someone who is too lazy to continue to do what they're supposed to do, will want things but won't get anything. I am not a sluggard and will not live as a sluggard. I will get what I want because I will trust and believe Your word Lord and I will be diligent.

I thank You Lord because the Holy Spirit in me will press me towards diligence! In Jesus name I pray. Amen!

Scripture References:

| Proverb 10:4 | Philippians 3:14 |
| Proverb 13:4 | Galatians 6:9 |

Father, I want to thank You this morning for Your protection from dangers seen and unseen. You have been protecting me all my life, sometimes it didn't feel like You were there, but even then You were protecting me from things and people that could have changed the course of my life for the worse or even taken my life.

Father sometimes Your protection is in the form of rejection, which is never a pleasant experience. Rejection makes my heart sink, causes me to feel inferior and makes me want to hide away because my feelings are hurt but, the reality is this: You use rejection as a tool to keep me safe from people, situations and circumstances that You know are not a part of Your call and plan for my life. Help me to see rejection as a gift from You.

Father, sometimes You use financial difficulty, illness or even the loss of a loved one to keep me safe and protect me from the schemes and plans of the enemy.

Lord, I declare that starting today I will not fight against Your protection of me. I will not grow angry, resentful or envious of others when You are at work covering, keeping and protecting me. Thank You for loving me so much You are willing to do whatever it takes to protect me from any and every one, or thing, that would harm me. You even protect me from me! Thank you Father!

In Jesus name I pray. Amen.

Scripture References:

| Jeremiah 24 | Ephesians 6:10 – 18 |
| Malachi 3:17 | I Peter 5:8 |

Father, Your Word says I should seek Your counsel first, but seeking Your counsel takes so much time. Seeking Your counsel means I have to stop what I'm doing, read Your Word, think about what You're conveying to me and then I have to internalize it. Lord seeking Your counsel takes effort and time.

The world system is constantly giving me its counsel without my asking for it. I don't have to stop what I'm doing; I can just keep watching TV, listening to the radio or reading books that have nothing to do with my relationship with You and the world system keeps pouring its counsel into my ears. It may not be good counsel but they just keep it coming!

I've come to the realization that the world system does not have my best interest at heart. I need Your counsel and the input from other people who operate in Godly wisdom because I'm tired of making decisions that don't give me what I want or worse, end up being bad decisions.

Lord God, I'm ready to make the effort to listen to Your counsel. I know that listening to You and those who operate in Your wisdom will propel me forward so I can make good decisions and become who You have purposed me to be from the beginning of time. Father God, help me! In Jesus name I pray and say, amen.

Scripture References:

King 22:5	Mark 1:35	Proverb 12:15
Matthew 7:13	Proverb 8:14	Proverb 15:22
Psalm 73:24	Hebrews 4:11 - 16	

Father God, as Your children climb out of the pit of the world system into the marvelous light of Your Son Jesus Christ, we need You to help us redefine success and failure.

Your children know what the world calls success; big homes, expensive cars and lots of money. Unfortunately, too often these "successes" come with relaxed morals and lacking ethics. We see it all the time on the news and even in some churches.

We have looked at others who have all the things the world calls success and tried to mimic them. That's why so many of us find ourselves broken and ashamed of what we've done and what we have become. Father, forgive us!

Lord, help us to seek after Your definition of success. Help us to look more and more like Jesus every day. Help us to obey Your Word even when we can't figure out what You're doing and, help us to seek after and fulfill the destiny You have planned for each of us.

Father help us replace our fear of earthly failure with the peace of being successful in You. Step by step and day by day help us to climb out of our spiritual pits so we can come into the full light of the Gospel of Jesus Christ. It is in the precious name of Jesus we pray and say Amen.

Scripture References:

Kings 18:5 – 7	I John 1:3, 6 – 7	II Timothy 2:3
Hebrews 13:5	Proverbs 24:19	
II Chronicles 26:5	Ephesians 1:3	

Father, when we realize how far we've allowed ourselves to fall into the pit falls of the world system, we feel hurt and disappointed with ourselves. Not only have we fallen into the financial pitfall of the world system but also the mental, emotion, physical and spiritual pitfalls. Thank You Lord for allowing us to go into the pits, but not allowing us to stay there!

Father, just like You were with Joseph when he went into the pit, You have been with us. You were with Joseph every step of the way during his time in Potiphar's home, while he was in prison and when he served in the court of Pharaoh; and You have been with, are still with and will continue to be with us.

Father, You didn't leave Joseph in the pit falls of his life and You won't leave us in our pitfalls. You brought Joseph out of his pits more powerful than when he went in to the pits and You will do the same thing for us if we have the character of Joseph.

Father You blessed Joseph because he operated in his gifts, no matter the circumstances he was facing. He was always honorable to his masters/bosses no matter how they treated him. Joseph always He handled the business affairs that were given to him with knowledge and truth and he always gave You, Lord God, the glory.

Father, while I am climbing out of the pit falls of the world system, help me to have the character of Joseph in all aspects of my life. It is in Jesus name I pray and say Amen.

Scripture References:

Genesis 37:23 – 24	Genesis 39:11 – 12	Genesis 40:8
Genesis 39:1 – 6	Genesis 39:20 – 23	Genesis 41:15 – 16

Holy God, it is my sincere desire to mature in my walk with You and my faith in You. I want to become all that You have purposed me to be and be an active participant as You fulfill every promise You have for me; but sometimes it seems that You allow things that concern me and cause me distress to linger in my life. It feels like no matter how much I pray, You still allow these issues to vex me. I know this is a part of the maturity process but Lord, it is so difficult!

Father I ask that You strengthen me so I do not allow the fear; fear of what other may think or say, fear of what I have done or, what I haven't done, to stop me from growing in You. Do not allow me to fall into the trap of pride and think I can come up with solutions on my own. Keep me mindful of how much I need You.

Father help me as I will allow patience and perseverance to have their perfect work. Remind me not move until I hear from You. I will rest, rely and recline my whole self on You, knowing that You not only care for me, but care about everything that concerns me. I pray in Jesus name. Amen.

Scripture References:

Psalm 55:22	Psalm 145:13	Hebrews 6:1
II Thessalonians 3:3	James 1:2 - 4	I Peter 5:6 - 7
Psalm 119:75	Ephesians 4:13	
II Timothy 2:11 - 13	James 2:17 - 18	

5 FAMILY

Father, Your Word says that if I remain in You and Your words remain in me, I can ask whatever I wish, and it will be given to me. Today I am asking You to bless families. There are marriages that need to be mended. There are parents ready to give up on their children because the actions of the children need to be corrected – grown children as well as the youngsters.

There are people who are working to take care of their children and aging parents. They need their parents' health restored, or for You to provide the way and the means for their parents to be properly care for, whether in their home or a facility.

There are families that are broken apart, unable to see each other on a regular basis, because of the current economic situation in our country. There are family businesses about to go under and people wondering when the next shoe is going to drop. There are families struggling with finances, some ready to throw in the towel. But my hope is in Your Word which says, if I pray, believing, I can have whatever I ask for and I am asking You to intervene for families.

God, there are people who need their family members to come to know You as their Lord and Savior. They have prayed for years asking for their loved ones' salvation. Father, please answer them now.

Lord, the families in our nation need a touch from You. No one else can make the necessary changes in their situations other than You. I am coming to You, casting my cares at Your feet, because I know You care for me. Lord, I give the families of this nation into Your love and care.

In Jesus' name I pray. Amen.

Scripture References:

John 15:7	Ephesians 6:1 – 4	I Peter 5:7
Acts 20:32	I Timothy 5:1 – 3	
Romans 1:29 – 31	Thessalonians 5:9	

Father, I thank You for blessing me with all spiritual blessings in Christ Jesus.

Your Word says skillful and godly wisdom is in my house, which means my life, home and family are built on and through the understanding of Your word. My home is made whole and it at peace through You. My home is established on a sound, solid and good foundation. By knowledge the rooms are filled with all precious and pleasant riches — great priceless treasure: love, peace, patience, kindness, generosity, goodness, and joy. Prosperity and welfare are in my house

Father in everything we do, we are working to take a righteous stand. Whatever You have given us to do, our family work at wholeheartedly, knowing that it's for Your glory and not for men.

Father, we love each other with Your kind of love; sometimes we don't show it, but we really do love each other and purpose to live in peace. Father, I give my home to Your charge. I entrust my house and the material gain, but most of all, the people who live in my home, into Your protection and care.

In Jesus' name I pray. Amen.

Scripture References:

Ephesians 1:3	Colossians 3:14, 15
Acts 16:31	Psalm 112:3
Proverbs 24:3, 4 (Amp)	Acts 20:32
Philippians 2:10, 11	Luke 6:48
Proverbs 15:6	Joshua 24:15
Colossians 3:23	Acts 4:11
Proverbs 12:7 (Amp)	

Father, for the last few weeks it seems like everything that can go wrong has gone wrong: money issues, housing concerns, relationship problems, and the list goes on. For those who go to work, it seems to be more difficult every day. Drama and trauma seems to be around every corner in the workplace. For those who own their own businesses, it seems that there aren't enough customers or clients to keep the company afloat. Forget about growth, just trying to maintain the contracts they have is enough of a challenge.

It seems no matter how much we pray, You don't hear us, or at least, You haven't answered. But we know You are still our hope and our help. So we ask you to fill our hearts with Your glory today. Let Your peace prevail in our lives. Allow Your joy to flow in our homes and please place Your grace and mercy over every aspect of our lives.

Everything may not go our way today, but You are still our God and You're still sovereign in everything You do. We will trust You.

We will trust that You have our best interest at heart. We will trust that You know what's best for our families. We will trust that You know what plans You have for us and the path we must take to fulfill those plans. We will trust Your love for us is the overriding factor for everything we experience today.

In Jesus' name I pray. Amen.

Scripture References:

Psalms 22:1 – 3	Proverbs 19:21	II John 1:3
Psalms 140:6 – 8	Romans 15:13	Psalms 37:4 – 6
Thessalonians 2:16	Jeremiah 29:11	Proverbs 3:5 – 6

Father, Your Word says what You have put together, let no man tear asunder. So often we think that means we can't divorce. But what that really means is that that we, as a married couple, cannot tear our marriage apart from the inside out. If we tear apart a union You have ordained, we are destroying the work of Your hands.

We can't destroy each other with our words and our attitudes. We can't destroy our children with our fighting and bickering. We can't destroy our families and isolate each other because of our selfish desires. We can't tear apart that which You, the Almighty God, have joined together.

Father, as we look at our union, help us to see our marriage for what it truly is in Your sight: a marital union of gifts, purposes and processes. You united our gifts to serve You in the world. You joined our purposes to give us what we need in order to pursue our individual and joint best in this life; and You brought together our processes so we could support each other as You move us from one level of glory to another. We need You and we need each other.

Father, bring about or restore the correct relationship between husbands and wives. Allow our lights to shine together so the world may see what it really means to be brought together by God.

In Jesus' name we pray. Amen.

Scripture References:

Matthew 19:6   Mark 10:9

Father God You don't make mistakes. When You put a two people together in marriage, You make a perfect match.

You don't falter and You can't fail. If there is failure it is in our human fragility. If one of us should stumble and fall, the other should be there to help him or her get up. If one should falter in his or her walk, the other should be there to pray for him or her. If one should fail in his or her duties or assignment, the other should be there to help heal his or her wounds until You, Father, can bring him or her back to wholeness.

Our duties and responsibilities to each other should override everything else, because we know that marriage is the only relationship You designed to look like our relationship with You. Marriage is the only earthly relationship designed to enable people to grow closer over the years rather than further apart. Marriage is the only relationship which is intended to last until death do us part and then, if we are in Christ, we are to spend our eternity as the bride to our eternal groom: Jesus Christ.

Father, bring about or restore the correct relationship between husbands and wives. Allow our lights to shine together so the world may see what it really means to be brought together by God.

In Jesus' name we pray. Amen.

Scripture References:

Matthew 19:6   Mark 10:9

Father, as Your children purpose to climb out of the muck and mire of the world system that we've put ourselves in, we're going to need Your divine help in the area of our finances. Too many of us are over extended and underwater with our credit, mortgages and other payments.

We confess we have not been good stewards of what You have given us. We have sought after things we really didn't need and as a consequence of our greed, we have placed ourselves in financial binds. Forgive us!

Father, we need Your wisdom regarding climbing out of these financial holes. Do we file bankruptcy? Do we go to credit counseling? Do we allow our homes to go into foreclosure? Do we allow other bills to go by the wayside while we pay off one debt at a time? We need an individual plan that fits each of our needs. Father, we are looking to You and You alone for our help.

Father God we know Your Word says You will supply all our of needs, not our greeds, according to Your riches in glory in Jesus Christ, so, even as we are climbing out of our financial holes, we are assured of Your blessings on our lives. Our needs will be met in Jesus name.

Lord God, we know Your Word says, "Let no debt remain outstanding, except the continuing debt to love one another…" As we climb out of this hole please help us help each other. Help us love one another and help us to encourage one another. Father, we need You now, more than ever. In Jesus name we pray. Amen.

Scripture References:

Job 12:13	Philippians 4:19	Luke 16:1 – 13
Romans 13:8	Proverbs 28:25	
Proverbs 15:27	Luke 12:15	

Father, I thank You that You have blessed me with all spiritual blessings in the heavenly realm in Christ Jesus.

Skillful and godly wisdom is in my house. My life, my home and my family are built on and by understanding. My home is made whole and is established on a good foundation. By knowledge the rooms are filled with all precious and pleasant riches — great priceless treasure; real treasures: love, peace, patience, kindness, generosity, goodness and joy.

In everything we do we are working to take a righteous stand. Prosperity and welfare are in my house in the name of Jesus.

Jesus is my Cornerstone. Jesus is Lord of my household. Jesus is Lord of my spirit, soul and body.

Lord, whatever you give us to do, we work at it heartily knowing that it's to Your glory and not for men.

We love each other with the Godly love. Sometime we don't show it, but we really do love each other, and we purpose to live in peace. Father I give my home to Your charge. I entrusted the house, the material gain, but most of all the people who live it my home into Your protection and care.

In Jesus name. Amen.

Scripture References:

Ephesians 1:3	Colossians 3:23	Luke 6:48
Acts 16:31	Proverbs 12:7 amp	Joshua 24:15
Proverbs 24:3,4 amp	Colossians 3:14,15	Acts 4:11
Philippians 2:10,11	Psalm 112:3	
Proverbs 15:6	Acts 20:32	

6 COMMUNITY

Father, I know Your word says that You know the plans you have for me: plans to do me good and not to harm me, plans to give me hope and a future hope. This isn't a promise just for me, but for everyone who calls on the name of Jesus. But, if I'm being honest, some days I don't feel like Your plan is working very well.

I look around and I see people losing everything. I see murder and mayhem, heartache and hardship, and I wonder if this really be Your plan. I've lost loved ones and friends. Good people, including myself and my family members, have lost homes, money, jobs, etc., while the unrighteous still prosper. Forgive me, but is this really a plan for my good? I feel like David when he said, "Why, O Lord, do You stand far off? Why do You hide Yourself in the time of trouble?"

But I will trust in Your unfailing love; my heart will rejoice in Your coming salvation. I know that at the right time and in the right season, if I don't give up, You will bless me and others in the Body of Christ with everything that is rightfully ours to inherit. I will not waver in my trust of You, but I will stand firm and see the deliverance of Your children.

Thank You for being a big enough God for me to be honest within my times of uncertainty, weakness and momentary despair. I will wait on You. I will be of good courage and I know You will strengthen my heart.

In Jesus' name I pray. Amen.

Scripture References:

| Jeremiah 29:11 | Psalms 10:1 | Psalms 13:5 |
| II Thessalonians 3:13 | Exodus 14:13 | Psalms 27:14 |

Father God, our children are returning to school. Whether they are entering kindergarten or returning to college, they are still our children. We love them and we pray for their safety, security and protection.

Father, the children we are praying for may be our biological children, step children, grandchildren, nieces, nephews, children in our guardianship, or just children that we know from the community. It makes no difference Lord; we pray for all of them because we know they are all Your divine creations.

We pray for their protection from unrighteous peer- pressure, gangs, drugs, and other vices that may drag them down the wrong path.

We pray that they develop good study habits, attract friends that are good for them and that they ask for help with their studies or other problems if they need help. Father, please let them know we are here for them and that You are always with them.

We also pray for their parents and guardians. Father, please let their parents and guardians know how important it is to become involved in their children's school lives. Help the parents and guardians carve out time to help with homework and give them the resources to get tutoring help for their children as needed. Father, impress upon the parents and guardians how important it is to talk to and listen to their children every day. Finally, let the parents and guardians know that they are not alone; we are here for them and so are You.

In Jesus' name we pray. Amen.

Scripture References:

| Mark 9:36 – 37 | Matthew 18:10 | Deut. 11:19 |
| Mark 10:13 – 16 | Ephesians 6:1 – 4 | |

Father, as our children return to school, we pray for the teachers, bus drivers, principals, cooks, cafeteria workers, administrators, janitors, school board members, coaches, deans, and anyone else who may come in direct or indirect contact with our students as they pursue their education.

Father, we thank You that Your word brings light and life. We are so grateful that Your word will perform what You set it out to do. So today, we speak Your word over everyone in a position of authority within school systems across our nation.

We pray that they use Your integrity, Your wisdom and Your understanding as they deal with our children. We pray that all wickedness, evilness, bigotry, and hatred be cut off from them and that they deal with our children in an upright manner.

Father God, we pray that if anyone in the school systems has an agenda of ill-will towards our children that You will stop their plans, render them useless and allow the person to be caught and brought to justice.

In Jesus' name we pray. Amen.

Scripture References:

I Peter 5:2	Proverbs 29:2
Acts 20:28	Galatians 6:9

Father, it seems that every time our nation takes a step towards recovery we take two steps backward. Fighting and bickering in the Senate and the House of Representatives seems to go on every day. Discord within the White House and disrespect for our nation's leader seems to abound. This is why we must put our hope and trust in You. Lord, in the midst of all these trials and difficulties, we look to You as our hope, our help and our strength.

So many people in our country need help. They need jobs, health insurance, protection from the environment and the conditions in which they are forced to live. Our lawmakers seem to have forgotten the citizens of our nation and have focused only on themselves. But, Father, even in the middle of this season of discontent, we can find our contentment and comfort in You.

Our faith looks up to You. We will lift our eyes to the hills from where our help comes from; our help comes from the Lord who created Heaven and Earth. There is no foe, not even our national leaders' egos that can withstand Your power and authority.

In this time of trouble, we are confident and boldly say, "God is our helper. He will answer the cry of His people from His holy hill." Hear us, oh Lord, and answer us right away. For without You, we have no hope; but, with You, all things are possible - even the healing of our land.

In Jesus' name, we pray and say, amen.

Scripture References:

Psalms 31:24	Psalms 121	- 15
Psalms 46:1	Isaiah 40:30 – 31	Micah 7:7
Psalms 33:18 – 21	II Chronicles 14:11	

Father, in the middle of all the turmoil in our lives, grant us peace.

Bring peace to our homes; stop the arguing, fussing and fighting among spouses. Stop children from disrespecting their parents and Father; stop us from harming ourselves with the words of our mouths.

We declare peace on our jobs; God, help us to stop worrying over whether we're going to have a job or not. Help us to realize that You are our provision, not our jobs. Help us to see the false sense of security we have when we depend on our jobs and not on You. Remind us that You gave us the jobs we currently have, and You will provide all of our needs according to Your riches in glory by Christ Jesus. All jobs belong to You!

Father, give us peace in our business dealings. Help us with our business plans. Help connect us to new clients and expand our client base. Help us listen to You as your direct our businesses in new directions.

And finally, Father, grant us inner peace – let the peace that surpasses all understanding, rest, rule and abide in our hearts.

Father, we will glorify and bless You. In Jesus' name we pray. Amen.

Scripture References:

Isaiah 26:3 – 4	Number 6:26	Proverbs 12:20
John 14:27	Proverbs 17:1	Philippians 4:7

Father, I look at the world today and I am broken hearted about all the murders and mayhem being leveled against our young people – honor students beaten to death for nothing, girls being gang raped at parties, boys being molested in locker rooms, and bullying so severe that children and young people without hope take their own lives. God, something has to happen.

Help me, Lord, to look at my life, my time, my skills, my talents, and my abilities to figure out how I can help. Is there an opportunity for me to mentor a young person? Is there a youth ministry I can get involved with? Is there a young person in my life that I can help groom and move in the right direction? Lord, what can I do to help?

Please God, don't let me hide behind the line of, "I don't have the money to do what I want to do." There are so many things I can do that wouldn't cost me anything. I can tutor a child in a subject in which they are struggling. I can coach a local sports team, even if I'm not a parent. I can talk to the young people at my church or at a local school. I can teach finances, sewing, music, carpentry, or how to stay away from drugs. Father, show me what I should do in order to have a positive impact on the young people of our country.

In Jesus' name I pray. Amen.

Scripture References:

| Matthew 25:37 – 40 | Matthew 19:14 | James 1:27 |

Father, I heard the number of American soldiers that commit suicide is going to sky-rocket higher than last year. That is so sad and unfortunate. It's not enough that our young men and women – who are also sons and daughters, husbands and wives, brothers and sisters – put themselves in harm's way for the safety and welfare of our nation. But we, as a nation, are not caring for them as we should while they protect us.

Father God, these circumstances anger and confuse me. We consider ourselves the greatest nation in the world, yet we are lax in caring for our defenders. Lord, this just shouldn't be. We'd rather spend more money on space exploration than on making sure our soldiers have the right equipment to do their jobs. It doesn't make a difference why we're at war, the fact is that we are, and we should do everything we can to take care of our soldiers.

Father, I pray for our soldiers today. Protect them mentally, physically, emotionally, spiritually, and financially. Father, cover them with Your wings of love and hide them in the time of danger. I put their safety in Your hands.

Lord, I also pray for our President, Congressmen and Senators, that they would be men and woman of wisdom and compassion when it comes to the affairs of our nation – specifically, when it comes to the affairs of our nation's defenders. Father, give them a heart to do what is right for those who are out there fighting to defend our laws, our way of life and our freedom.

In Jesus' name I pray. Amen.

Scripture References:

Psalms 144:1 – 2	Isaiah 6:8
John 15:13	I Timothy 2:1 – 6

Lord, as the temperature begins to drop and I see the multitude of homeless people on the streets, I think of the scripture that says, "When I was naked you clothed me. When I was hungry you fed me and when I was in prison you visited me". I realize that the majority of so-called Christians have really fallen short of our jobs.

It's not the government that is supposed to take care of our brothers and sisters, it's us – those who are in the Body of Christ and say they have a relationship with You. We are responsible for the care of those who are lost, societies that are least and people who are considered "less than." Forgive us for not caring enough for our brothers and sisters to feed, clothe and visit them in their time of need.

Help us reach them, teach them skills and help them become productive members of society. Help us to help up, not just help out.

In Jesus' name I pray. Amen.

Scripture References:

James 2:14 – 17	Luke 14:12 – 14	James 2:1 – 3

Father, today I turn my eyes and attention to the plight of the citizens of the world that deal with war, death and destruction on a daily basis. Let us not forget that they are citizens of the world and, as such, they deserve our prayers and help.

Most of them had nothing except their family and friends before war broke out in their countries, their cities and towns were overrun by terrorist or a natural disaster hit their communities. Now many of them have nothing at all. God, help us not give lip service to the current welfare of our brothers and sisters; but let us consider what it would   be like to lose our mother, father, sisters, brothers, sons, and daughters, who were with us one moment and gone the next.

Let us think of the mental devastation that those who live in war-torn countries must be going through – knowing that what little they had, and the things they cherished, have been buried under the rubble of the buildings in which they were stored, never to be recovered again.

Pictures, mementos, trophies, and awards of accomplishment that accounted for so many moments of someone's life, are lost in seconds. My God, help me understand true compassion. Help me urge my neighbors, children's schools, churches, and community groups to organize for the purpose of bringing about real change in the lives of many who have lost so much.

Father, give us a heart for the people. In Jesus' name I pray. Amen.

Scripture References:

James 1:27	James 2:14 – 17
Deuteronomy 15:11	Proverbs 29:7

Father, I think about the inequality that so many still have to suffer. So many people are still burdened under the yoke of bondage, required to bow down to a master that doesn't care about them, and are still searching for a way to freedom.

So many people have fought for the freedom of the human body and mind, but Jesus died for the freedom of the human spirit and everlasting life. While some marched in the streets of Alabama, Mississippi, Johannesburg, Beijing, and Cairo bringing a message of change and hope, Jesus marched the streets of Jerusalem, Jericho and Capernaum being the change and hope the people wanted and needed. Many people, who have led marches, sit ins and lock outs, were killed by bullets because of their work; but Jesus willingly laid down his life on a cross as his completed work against everything evil.

Father, help me to be a beacon of light that shows people that Your Son is the way out of slavery and bondage to sin and death. That in Jesus there is life, wholeness, hope and peace.

Lord, as I work to celebrate the life and accomplishments of many people who forged a path for freedom, never allow me to forget to work to fulfill the call on my life that came from You. Your plans for me will give me a hope and a future. Help me to focus and fulfill the call and plan You have for me just as Abraham Lincoln, Mahatma Gandhi, Rev. Dr. Martin Luther King, Jr., Mikhail Gorbachev, Nelson Mandela and Jesus fulfilled their purposes.

In Jesus' name I pray. Amen.

Scripture References:

| Romans 8:12–17 | Romans 8:28–30 | Romans 11:29–32 |

Father, we thank You that this nation is blessed because our God is the Lord and we are the people You have chosen for Your inheritance. It saddens me, Lord, to see us fighting and tearing our nation apart from the inside out. We don't have to worry about terrorist attacks from other nations; we have people in leadership who are terrorizing our very own citizens.

Lord, Your word is clear that we are to take care of the orphans, the widows and those who are in need. Help us Father not to be a nation run by greed verses need. Help us, Father, not to mistreat our fellow citizens who have less than the rich rulers. Help us to show true Christian love and do unto others as we would want others to do unto us.

We release Your Truth into every realm of life in this nation so that men may say, "Surely this great nation is a wise and understanding people."

In Jesus' name I pray. Amen.

Scripture References:

| Psalm 33:12 | James 1:27 | Matthew 7:12 |

Father, this morning I pray for all the leaders in our country. The president, senators, congressmen and women,

U.S. Supreme Court justices and everyone who has been privileged to be in a place of authority that allows them to make decisions that should bring about the greater good for all people.

Lord, I pray that they will allow Your love, Your wisdom and Your knowledge to rest, rule and dictate what they do and how they do it. Remind them that they have been put in their positions by the common working class people of this nation and it is their responsibility as leaders to care for all of our nation's citizens.

Father, protect our leaders from hate groups: violent and ignorant men and women – many who call themselves Christians or Muslims but are filled with hate – who want to bring terror to our country. Touch them with the knowledge of Your love so that they may know what it is to love like Christ. Please watch over our nation and keep our citizens safe.

In Jesus' name I pray. Amen.

Scripture References:

Isaiah 9:6 – 7

Father, things seem to be getting worse instead of better. Our leaders are at each other's throats, citizens are pursuing violence as a way to get their points across and people in our country are still losing jobs, their homes and their hope. The stress that can build through all these facts is enough to make an average person give up.

But we're not average! We are a royal priesthood, great and mighty to achieve great things in Your name and through Your power. So we shall press on. We will not grow weary of doing good, but we will show the love of Christ everywhere we go. We will not faint, but we will allow our lives to be a beacon of hope to those who have lost their way.

We will move forward in victory! In Jesus' name we pray. Amen.

Scripture References:

Isaiah 40:30 – 31   Galatians 6:9

Father, You have given me something far more precious than silver or gold. You have given me friends and family. People who watch over me and take care of me. You've put people in my life who pray for me without my asking, and think about me just because. I have people in my life who have my best interest at heart.

So today, Lord, I want to pray for my friends and family. Please bless them with everything they need for rich, well- rounded lives. Meet every need they have and show them how much You love them by being there for them at all times.

Most of all, Father, give them friends and family members to surround them with love, hope and compassion just like my friends and family surround me.

In Jesus' name I pray. Amen.

Scripture References:

Psalm 122:8	Proverbs 18:24	John 15:13

Father, it seems that with all the media coverage about Congress and the Senate fighting with the White House, we have forgotten about the people who are being adversely affected by the greed of big business and big government's neglect.

There are families who have owned businesses for four and five generations that are going to have to close their doors. There are people who have been employed by companies that are unable to retain them, because there's no work and, possibly, no work for years to come.

Lord, it seems that we have forgotten the people who lost their lives because of street violence, wars and hopelessness. Their families are in mourning and will grieve the loss of their loved ones for a long time.

Today, Lord God, I pray for the families whose lives have been altered because of the on-going violence in the United States and abroad. Father, I pray for justice for them. I pray that You would return to them everything they've lost: peace of mind, a sense of security and joy.

pray for the people who are working to clean up the mess: our policemen, EMTs, soldiers, and firefighters. Father, give them wisdom. Lord, the earth is Yours and the fullness thereof; help us take better care of what You've given us to oversee. Help us to see the needs of our brothers and sisters, and give to them in order to support them in their time of need.

In Jesus' name I pray. Amen.

Scripture References:

Psalm 34:10	James 1:27
Matthew 6:25 – 27	Matthew 25:36 – 40

Father, in a time when we seem to have lost sight of what it means to love one another in spite of our differences, help me to be a beacon of light that shines out to mankind.

There is still good in our nation, but it seems that the foolishness of hatred, bigotry and bias has covered up the good. We hear words of hate, doom and condemnation loud and clear, but seldom do we hear words of thankfulness, consideration and love.

Help those of us who stand for peace, love and working together prevail against the work of the haters. Help those of us who call ourselves Christians to show the love of Christ and not the hate of the world. Father, we need Your love, Your guidance and Your direction during these difficult times.

In Jesus' name we pray. Amen.

Scripture References:

Timothy 3:1 – 5   Galatians 6:9

Father, I pray for people the world over who are suffering because of the loss of a loved one to gun violence. Lord, You control all things, so I come to You to ask that You would allow Your peace to flood the survivors' hearts and minds.

Father, guns are not the problem. The hearts and the minds of the people with the guns are the problem. Are while all these issues are raging around us, those of us who call ourselves Your children are sitting back and doing very little to bring about change in our communities and neighborhoods. We have barricaded ourselves in buildings we call "churches," and in traditions, to the point where we are no good to the lost, the least and the less than.

There are some families who have nothing, but the institute of the church is reluctant to reach out to them because it will cost money and time. There are families who need common household items: food, soap, laundry detergent, etc., so that they can send their children to school. But we, the "Church," turn a blind eye to their needs. Forgive us!

Father, help us love others the way You love us: without judgment, without criticism, without complaint, and without comparisons. God, please help us be the Body of Christ in this world.

In Jesus' name I pray. Amen.

Scripture References:

Romans 7:4	Jeremiah 7:1 – 3	Timothy 5:4
Romans 12:3	James 1:26 – 27	

Father God, today I pray for those who can't seem to handle everyday life without help from drugs. Legal and illegal drugs have become a part of their lives to help handle the normal rigors of living. You did not design us to be dependent on anything or anyone other than You.

Father, I pray that You would lose those who are addicted to anything; drugs, alcohol, sex, work, overspending or anything else from the bondage they are in, release them into Your love, peace, joy and contentment. Allow them to find a sweet existence in You., Help them release the stress they are feeling by learning to rest in and rely on You. Help them realize that nothing is impossible with You, but everything is done in accordance with Your time and in Your way.

Father, help relieve our nation from its addictions of all kinds.

In Jesus' name I pray. Amen.

Scripture References:

Isaiah 9:6	Philippians 4:7
Romans 15:13	Hebrews 13:20

Father, today I link my prayer with millions of others around the world who are praying for war-torn countries. Father, they need You to intervene on their behalf. No matter where we live, we are all Your children and You love each of us equally.

Father, we pray for those who have lost loved ones. Allow them time to grieve and mourn their loss, but then turn to You. Be their loving Father who is full of tender mercy.

Father, we pray for those who have lost all of their material goods: their home, clothes, car, and jobs. Losses like those can push some people over the edge, but Lord we ask that You guard their hearts and their minds as they move through their tragedies one day at a time.

Father, we pray for the leaders of other nations and the leaders of the United States. Help them to reach out and help the lost, the least and the less than in this time of great turmoil. Father, be our peace.

In Jesus' name we pray. Amen.

Scripture References:

Thessalonians 1:3

Father, Your word tells us to pray for those in leadership and power. Therefore I come before You today to pray for our president, senators and congressmen and women, because although they're in power, they are acting like spoiled children.

Father, please help our leaders to see that the road they are leading us down is a damned one. Just as the country is coming to a place where new, small businesses are being created and people going back to work, some of our leadership wants to take us backwards and put small businesses and employment in jeopardy for millions of Americans.

All the posturing and all the politics is just for show. There is no validity for the American people in what some of our leadership wants to do. Please give our leaders compassionate hearts to see beyond their own fat bank accounts and see into the lives of everyday working Americans who just want to go to work, feed their families, pay their rent and mortgages, and save a little for a rainy day.

I know, Lord, that we vote politicians into office because we think they will do the job we want them to do, but my hope is in You because I know You'll always be the God I need You to be. Thank you.

In Jesus' name I pray. Amen.

Scripture References:

Hebrews 13:17

Father, it has gotten to the point I hate watching the news. Killings are mounting up daily, and every day we see citizens killing citizens, police killing citizens and citizens killing police. It is just too much!

All types of movements are springing up and saying this life matters and that life matters, as if You didn't make all life and all life doesn't matter to You. Forgive us Father! Lord, for those of us in the body of Christ who have been given the charge of loving You and loving mankind, help us to see human life; which born or unborn, Black, White, Hispanic, Asian or other, is important to You.

When Jesus came to die for the sins of the world, it wasn't just for Jewish sinners, Muslim sinners or Christian sinners. He didn't just die for sexual sins or moral sins. Jesus loved all sinners enough to die for all our sins. Forgive us Father for acting like, and treating others as if their sins are greater than our own. For we have all sinned and fallen short of Your glory.

You have told us to love each other to the point that we are willing to lay down our lives for theirs. You did not tell us to judge them by their lifestyle, their tattoos or their hairstyles. Your word says, *"Dear friends, let us love one another, for love comes from God. Everyone who loves has been born of God and knows God. Whoever does not love does not know God, because God is love."*

Father, increase our hearts capacities to love others like You love us; without finding fault, without holding our sins against us and without treating us as outcasts. You loved us back to wholeness in You; help us do the same for someone else that needs You as much as we need You.

In Jesus' name we pray. Amen!
Scripture References:

| John 3:16 – 18 | Romans 5:8 | I John 4:7 – 8 |
| Romans 3:22 – 24 | I John 3:16 | |

Heavenly Father, our most gracious and loving God, I pray asking that You would abundantly bless everyone reading this prayer and their families. Please bless them spiritually, mentally, emotionally, physically and financially. They need a five-fold blessing!

Father Your word says that with the measure that we've measured out so shall it be measured back to us. Your word says that as we sow so shall we also reap. Your word clearly states that if we give, it will be given unto us; in good measure, pressed down, shaken together and running over.

Father, I ask right now that You would release spiritual, mental, emotional, physical and/or financial blessing into the homes, the hands and into the lives of everyone who is reading this prayer. You know exactly what each family needs. You are our Jehovah Jireh, our provision already met. Everything our families need has already been provided by You.

Father we are asking for the manifestation in the earth of what has already been ordained in heaven. Out of Your bounty in heaven, pour forth everything we need in accordance with Your riches in glory in Christ Jesus. We stand in agreement with each other and with Your word. In Jesus name we pray. Amen!

Scripture References:

Malachi 3:6 – 12	Galatians 6:7 – 8	Mark 11:22 – 24
Romans 12:3	Matthew 18:18 – 19	James 5:16
Matthew 6:10	Philippians 4:19	Luke 6:38
II Corinthians 9:16	Mark 4:22 – 24	
Matthew 16:19	James 3:18	

Father, I know so many people who are suffering financially right now. I know for some people their financial problems are their own making; over spending, using their credit cards without a plan or a thought and being a glutton when it comes to material things.

For others Lord, their financial problems came about because of loss of job, downsized salary, college for their children, or maybe for themselves, divorce or illness. No matter the reason for the financial stress and stretch they find themselves in, I pray that You will deliver them out of everyone.

We know when we go after money rather than coming after You, and Your will for our lives, we show a love of money, which is the root of all evil. This is because we know that You will supply all our needs according to the riches of Your glory in Jesus Christ. We know that Your word says that money answers all things, but we are to seek Your kingdom first, and everything else we need will be added to us.

Father, in the midst of the financial pressures that Your people are experiencing, please help us stay focused on You and Your will for our lives. Our hope is in You. We need You to be true to Your word and provide us as only You can. In Jesus' name we pray. Amen.

Scripture References:

Ecclesiastes 10:19	Philippians 4:19
I Timothy 6:10	Matthew 6:33

7 HOLIDAYS

Father, today I pray a simple prayer during this Thanksgiving season. In the midst of shopping, cooking and eating, please help me not to forget what I am most thankful for: Your commitment me.

You have committed to be my Father, my God, my Savior, and my Lord. Thank you!

In Jesus' name I pray. Amen.

Scripture References:

Lev. 26:12	Ezek. 37:27	I John 3:1
Jer. 32:38	James 1:27	

Father, what I'm about to pray may seem odd to those who are entrenched in this world system, but I want to be a good steward of everything You've given me, even during the Christmas season.

Father, this world system wants us to overspend, go into debt and purchase a lot of things we don't need. It wants us to operate out of a spirit of greed and not out of knowledge of need. It wants us to forget why we are celebrating Christmas, which is to celebrate the birth of our Lord and Savior.

Lord God, I want You to help me move out of the commercialism of Christmas and into the true meaning of the holiday. Help me to serve others. Christ came as a baby, not be served but to serve the world. Help me, Lord, to serve others during this time of year. Help me not be compelled to do more or spend more unnecessarily, but help me to show someone the light of the gospel of Jesus Christ.

In Jesus' name I pray. Amen.

Scripture References:

Matthew 20:28	Isaiah 9:6 - 7	I Peter 5:2

Father, during this season of love, joy and peace, please help me to remember those who need to know Your love in their lives through the touch of my hands.

I need to touch people who are confined to their beds of affliction in their homes, in convalescent homes, hospitals, and long-term care facilities. Father, they need to know Your love through me. Help me seek out and help people in homeless shelters, people who need to eat in community kitchens, and those whose only source of food is a local food pantry.

Father, You said it is my responsibility to go out and find those who are in need and show them the love of Christ. Help me, Lord, to come out of my selfishness and reach out to those in need and give them the real meaning of the season: Your love through Jesus Christ.

Let me not think about how they can return my kindness, but allow me to do for them knowing they can't return anything to me. Help me not to do it just for this month, or the next few weeks, but help me keep this spirit of giving all year long.

Help me, Lord, to be selfless like Christ, for this is the real reason for the season.

In Jesus' name. Amen.

Scripture References:

Matthew 25:34 – 40

Father, during this holiday season, help me let Your light shine so that others may know the real Reason for the Season. Help me remember that Jesus was born into the earth because of Your great love for mankind. Help me show Your love to everyone: to my friends and family, to those who are in need, and even to those whose philosophy I don't like or agree with.

Your love, care and concern for us is unconditional; help me to show Your unconditional love.

In Jesus' name I pray. Amen.

Scripture References:

I Corinthians 13:4 – 7	Luke 6:27
John 3:16	I John 4:7 – 11

Father, as I take the time to look back over the last year, I realize I need to ask for Your forgiveness. Last year I didn't focus on You. I didn't focus on the goodness or the kindness You showed me every day.

I was focused on the things of this world – my financial shortfalls, the things I wanted that didn't seem to come my way. I focused on what I don't have much more than I focused on the good You provided to me every day. For this, I am sorry and ask for Your forgiveness.

Lord, this year I commit to being more thankful. I will be thankful for Your love, Your goodness and Your provisions. I may not have everything I want, but You promised to supply my needs, not my greed. I may not have what I think someone else has, but I know You have my best interest at heart. I may not be able to accomplish everything I think I want to, but help me to accomplish everything You purpose me to do.

Lord, I commit to focusing on You, Your love and the mercy You show me and my family. I will purpose to be in a position of praising You for everything I have every day, and I will not complain as much this year as I did last year. I will allow Your grace and mercy to speak out of my life and into the world so that people can come to know You for themselves.

In Jesus' name I pray. Amen

Scripture References:

| Philippians 4:19 | Ephesians 2:4 – 5 | Numbers 23:19 |
| Hebrews 12:28 – 29 | I John 1:9 | Romans 12:2 |

Father, as I begin to make plans and set goals for myself, my family and my professional life for this year, don't let me forget that my plans must take a backseat to the plans You have for me. Nothing I plan is going to be better for me than what You have already ordained.

know everything is not going to go the way I want it to go, but I am sure that everything will go the way You've ordained it to go. Help me to mature to the points that when what You've ordained overrides my plans, I do not fret, complain or grumble. But instead, I rest in the knowledge that You have my best interest at heart.

You planned my perfect path long ago, and You know what's best for me. You will improve me until I fit into Your plan for me. Thank you, Lord, for caring enough about me that You planned for my greatness in the land of the living.

In Jesus' name I pray. Amen.

Scripture References:

Proverbs 19:21   Psalms 65:9   Isaiah 25:1

Father, we celebrate the resurrection of Your son, our Savior, Jesus the Christ every day. We need to remember how thankful we are for what Jesus did on our behalf. We should be ever mindful of the ultimate sacrifice He made for us.

Today, Father, help us to remember that we also must sacrifice on behalf of others. You called us to look after the orphans and the widows. Help us to have a heart for those who can't do for themselves, just like Your son had the heart to do for us what we couldn't do for ourselves.

Help us to treat others the way Jesus treated us: with a love that considers the plight of others more than our selfish desires.

In Jesus' name I pray. Amen.

Scripture References:

John 13:34 – 35	Romans 6:9 – 11	Corinthian 13:11
John 20:1 – 10	Romans 12:10	
Romans 5:8	James 4:1 – 3	

During my everyday comings and goings – in the midst of shopping, cooking, working, meeting with friends and interacting with my family, help me not to forget what I am most thankful for: Your commitment to me.

You have committed to be my Father, my God, my Savior, and my Lord. Thank you!

In Jesus' name I pray. Amen.

Scripture References:

Lev. 26:12	Ezek. 37:27	I John 3:1
Jer. 32:38	James 1:27	

During my everyday comings and goings – in the midst of shopping, cooking, working, meeting with friends and interacting with my family, help me not to forget what I am most thankful for: Your commitment to me.

You have committed to be my Father, my God, my Savior, and my Lord. Thank you!

In Jesus' name I pray. Amen.

Scripture References:

Leviticus 26:12	Ezekiel 37:27	I John 3:1
Jeremiah 32:38	James 1:27	

Thank You Lord for giving me a heart to daily renew my mind in Your word. I will submit myself to You as I make a break from my old life. This is what the Lenten season is all about; breaking out of the old to become newer in Christ and allowing You to propel me forward in the sanctification process.

Father I know that as I press to be more like Jesus I'm going to be like a child who's learning to walk. I'm going stand, titter and fall. I'm going to falter, fail and come up short of what I had hoped to accomplish, but that's okay! This too is a part of the sanctification process. Thank you for Your forgiveness! So, here I go, out to conquer my old self one baby step at a time! In Jesus name. Amen.

Scripture References:

John 17:17, 19	Romans 12:2	James 4:7 – 10
I Thessalonians 5:23	I Peter 1:1 – 2	I John 1:7 – 10

Father God, during Lenten season I am always concerned about what I'm going to give up so I can show You how sorry I am for the sins I've committed since the last Lenten season. I use this one thing as the scape goat for all my shortcomings and sins.

I use this season as a time for complaining about what I'm not doing or can't do. I use this season as a time to compare my sacrifice to someone else's. Never have I used this season to compare my sacrifice to the price You paid for my salvation by sacrificing Your son. Forgive me for trivializing what You've done for me.

Father during this Lenten season let me incorporate more of Your son's character. Let me love more like Jesus. Let me forgive more like Jesus. Let me show compassion and grace to others like Jesus shows to me. Let me think of others more than myself, like Jesus did when He died on the cross for my sins. During this Lenten season, help I be more like Jesus. I pray in Jesus name. Amen.

Scripture References:

Numbers 7:16	Acts 11:23	Matthew 18:21 – 22
Mark 11:25	Zechariah 12:10	James 5:11
I Samuel 15:22	Ephesians 5:2	John 15:12
John 3:16 – 18	Matthew 9:36	
Psalm 51:17	Colossians 3:13	

Father, I began this Lenten Season as a journey to know You better. Some days I stayed the course, other days I strayed away allowing other things to distract me from my journey. No matter what, I learned that getting and maintaining a relationship with You through Jesus Christ is a lifelong journey. I will mess up along the way, but if I stay the course, I'm still on the right path.

Along the way to finding out more about You, I found out more about me. As much as I love you, I still fall short but You knew I wasn't going to be perfect, that's why You sent Your Son to be my ransom; to take all my sins and carry them to the cross.

As much as I want to do everything You want me to do, my faith is lacking in so many areas. That's why You sent Jesus, as a man, to show me the importance of prayer and obedience. In His humanity Jesus didn't want to go to the cross, but out of obedience to You, He went anyway.

want to be bold and courageous in the things You have purposed for me to do but I allow the things of my past to interfere with my future. That's why You sent Your Son to be the anointment for Your forgiveness for me, one time for all time. Now, I need to forgive myself the way You forgive me.

On this Good Friday I look at the cross that Jesus died on a little differently. It wasn't something He did for everyone; it is something He did just for me. Thank you Jesus for dying in my place and becoming sin for me so I can have everlasting life through You. I pray in Jesus name. Amen.

Scripture References:

Matthew 26:36 – 39	Romans 6:12 – 14	Romans 10:4
Romans 10:8 - 11	Hebrews 9:14 - 15	Hebrews 10:8 – 10

Father the more I purpose to walk in Your light, the more difficult things become. The more I try to be upright, the more other people try to pull me down to their level of hurt, pain and unrighteous living. I know in the end I win but the struggle is real!

Lord, as I face another day my hope is in Your integrity and Your uprightness. No matter what may come my way or what I may face today, my hope is in You. This may mean that my plans and the schedule I have set for myself is only a suggestion. Help me to recognize the way You have laid out for me today.

As I purpose to fulfill Your plans for me today my knees may grow weak from standing on Your word and Your promises; strengthen me. My way may grow dim; guide me. My path may look like its falling away; affirm my steps. My hope is in You all day long! In Jesus name I pray. Amen!

Scripture References:

Psalm 33:18, 20, 22	Isaiah 40:31	Micah 7:7 – 8
Psalm 119:105	Numbers 23:19	II Peter 3:9
Psalm 130:5	Lamentations 3:25	
Isaiah 55:10 – 11	Hebrews 11:11	

Father, I am three months into the New Year and the things I promised I would make a priority, coupled with my desire to look more like Jesus, are beginning to feel like a job more than a blessing. I struggle with choices. I beat myself up when I make a mistake. Sometimes I feel like the changes I am trying to make are making things worse instead of better.

The guilt I feel when I miss the mark and shame for falling short are beginning to take their toll on me mentally and emotionally. I'm starting to listen to those voices in the back of my mind telling me the changes I want to make aren't worth it.

Help me to remember that You don't condemn me. In fact, because of what Jesus has done, I am set free from condemnation. You didn't create me to be a robot; mechanical, living without feelings or emotions and perfect in all I do. No, You created me to be who I am, made perfect through my relationship with Your perfect son, Jesus Christ.

Father help me not to be so hard on myself. Help me to appreciate the journey You have for me. Help me to rely on the finished work of Jesus as my perfection. In Jesus name I pray. Amen.

Scripture References:

Samuel 22:31 – 33	Colossians 1:28
Romans 8:1 – 2	Hebrews 10:1 – 10

Father on Martin Luther King, Jr's birthday I think about the inequality that so many still have to suffer. So many are still burdened under the yoke of bondage, still required to bow down to a master that doesn't care about them and still searching for a way to freedom.

While Dr. King fought for the freedom of the human body and mind, Jesus died for the freedom of the human spirit and everlasting life. While Dr. King marched in the streets of Alabama, Mississippi and Illinois bringing a message of hope, Jesus marched the streets of Jerusalem, Jericho and Capernaum being the hope for people. While Dr. King died by an assassins bullet because of his work, Jesus willing laid down his life on a cross as his completed work against everything evil.

Father, help me to be a beacon of light that shows people that Your son is the way out of slavery and bondage to sin and death. That in Jesus there is life and wholeness, hope and peace.

Lord, as I work to celebrate the life and accomplishments of Dr. King, never allow me to forget that Rev. Dr. King worked to fulfill the call on his life that came from You, just as Jesus died to fulfill the plan You had for him; a plan to give me a hope and a future. Help me to focus on the call and the plan you have for me, and help me work to fulfill that call and plan just as Dr. King and Jesus did.

In Jesus' name. Amen.

Scripture References:

| Genesis 1:27 | Romans 2:11 |
| Acts 10:34 | Galatians 3:26 - 29 |

ABOUT THE AUTHOR

First Lady Anita Patterson Wamble always wanted to be a teacher, but her mother told her teaching was "beneath her." So she went to the University of California at Berkeley to earn a degree in pharmaceutical research because she wanted to be to develop a chemical compound so people all over the world could have clean water. However, God had another plan.

Despite First Lady Anita's academic pursuits, the hunger to teach never subsided. In 1994, she accepted her call to the ministry. Over the past 19 years, she has taught Sunday school, led Education Ministries at various churches, preached to hundreds in DC, Maryland and Virginia, and led numerous workshops. Her ministry is not a surprise considering she hails from a family that has 23 active ministers in various denominations ranging in offices from local pastors to Bishops.

Several years ago, the Oakland, CA native got frustrated seeing people struggle with simple issues of everyday life. They struggled not because they did not believe in the word of God, but because they didn't know how to apply it to their lives. In 1999 First Lady Anita began writing "It's Still Relative – The Word of God for Today's World." "It's Still Relative" was written for the every person who has ever read the Bible and walked away saying, "I don't get it." The book was published in 2005 and is available through Amazon.

First Lady Anita is married to Pastor Marvin Wamble They have three children, Alicia Williams, Julian and Jenise Wamble and two grandchildren. For over 10 years First Lady Anita served as a

Certified Lay Servant and now serves as a Certified Lay Minister (CLM) in the United Methodist Church. She is employed by FEMA as a Program Analyst.

First Lady Anita has not abandoned her search for a water purification compound. She continues to teach about the purity of the living water – Jesus Christ.

Her favorite scripture is Ephesians 4:11 – 13: "It was He who gave some to be apostles, some to be prophets, some to be evangelists, and some to be pastors and teachers, to prepare God's people for works of service, so that the body of Christ may be built up until we all reach unity in the faith and in the knowledge of the Son of God and become mature, attaining to the whole measure of the fullness of Christ."